Basic Skills for the
TOEFL® iBT

Moraig Macgillivray
Kayang Gagiano

Compass
Publishing

Reading 2

Basic Skills for the TOEFL® iBT 2

Reading

Moraig Macgillivray · Kayang Gagiano

© 2008 Compass Publishing

Project Editor: Liana Robinson
Acquisitions Editor: Emily Page
Content Editor: Michael Jones
Copy Editor: Alice Wrigglesworth
Contributing Writers: Edaan Getzel
Consultants: Lucy Han, Chanhee Park
Cover/Interior Design: Dammora Inc.

email: info@compasspub.com
http://www.compasspub.com

ISBN: 978-1-59966-157-5

10 9 8 7 6 5 4 3 2 1
10 09 08

Contents

Introduction to the TOEFL® iBT

What is the TOEFL® test?

The TOEFL® iBT test (Test of English as a Foreign Language Internet-based test) is designed to assess English proficiency in non-native speakers who want to achieve academic success as well as effective communication. It is not meant to test academic knowledge or computer ability; therefore, questions are always based on material found in the test.

The TOEFL® iBT test is divided into four sections:
- Reading
- Speaking
- Listening
- Writing

TOEFL® Scores

TOEFL® scores can be used for:
- Admission into university or college where instruction is in English
- Employers or government agencies who need to determine a person's English ability
- English-learning institutes who need to place students in the appropriate level of English instruction

It is estimated that about 4,400 universities and other institutions require a certain TOEFL® test score for admission.

The exact calculation of a TOEFL® test score is complicated and not necessary for the student to understand. However, it is helpful to know that:
- Each section in the Internet-based test is worth 30 points
- The highest possible score on the iBT is 120 points
- Each institution will have its own specific score requirements

✻ It is very important to check with each institution individually to find out what its admission requirements are.

Registering for the TOEFL® iBT

Students who wish to take the TOEFL® test must get registration information. Registration information can be obtained online at the ETS website. The Internet address is www.ets.org/toefl.

The website provides information such as:
- testing locations
- identification requirements
- registration information
- costs
- other test preparation material
- test center locations

This information will vary depending on the country in which you take the test. Be sure to follow the requirements carefully. If you do not have the proper requirements in order, you may not be able to take the test. Remember that if you register online, you will need to have your credit card information ready.

Introduction to the Reading Section of the TOEFL® iBT

In the reading section of the TOEFL® test, you will be required to read 3–5 passages on varying topics. After each passage, you will answer 12–14 questions that test your ability to:
- understand vocabulary
- recognize sentence structure
- determine factual information
- determine implied information
- recognize the writer's intention

You will not be permitted to see the questions until after you have read the passage. While answering the questions, you will be permitted to look back at the reading. You do not need any previous knowledge on the topic in order to answer the questions correctly.

Passage Types:

1. Exposition—material that provides information about or an explanation of a topic
2. Argumentation—material that presents a point of view about a topic and provides supporting evidence in favor of a position
3. Narrative—an account of a person's life or a historical event

Reading Question Types:

Most questions will be multiple-choice questions. The following list explains the types and number of each type of question per passage. Questions may not appear in this order.

Question Type	Number	Description
Vocabulary	3–4	Choose the best meaning of a word or phrase
Reference	0–1	Identify the noun to which a pronoun is referring
Factual Information	2–4	Select details or facts provided in the passage
Negative Fact	1	Identify details or facts NOT provided, or NOT true according to the passage
Sentence Simplification	1	Choose the best answer to demonstrate your understanding of a sentence and your ability to analyze its meaning
Inference	0–1	Draw an inference from the passage by choosing an answer that is not actually said in the passage, but is implied or can be inferred
Rhetorical Purpose	1–2	Identify why the writer has mentioned something in a certain way or in a certain place
Insert Text	1	Insert a sentence into the most appropriate place in the passage
Summary	0–1	Choose the sentences that best summarize the entire passage
Table	0–1	Categorize major ideas or important information from the passage

Most questions are worth 1 point each, however Summary questions are worth 2 points and Table questions are worth 3-4 points.

Test management:

- Questions cannot be viewed until after the passage has been read.
- You can return to previous questions you may wish to revise or recheck by using the Review icon at the top of the screen.
- You will be allowed to study the reading as you attempt the questions.
- There is a glossary included for some words.
- When reading passages, ask yourself the following important questions:
    - ⇨ What is the main idea of the passage?
    - ⇨ How is the main idea developed/supported in the passage?
    - ⇨ What is the main point/role of each paragraph?
- You have 60–100 minutes to read the passages and answer 12–14 questions per passage. This usually means approximately 20 minutes per passage and set of questions. Try to pace yourself accordingly. The recommended reading speed would be approximately 100–150 words per minute. Therefore, you should try to read the passages in this book at that speed.
- For each set of questions, first answer all of the questions that you can answer easily. You can then go back and answer questions that are more difficult if you have time.

Introduction to the *Basic Skills for the TOEFL® iBT* series

Basic Skills for the TOEFL® iBT is a 3-level, 12-book test preparation series designed for beginning-level students of the TOEFL® iBT. Over the course of the series, students build on their current vocabulary to include common TOEFL® and academic vocabulary. They are also introduced to the innovative questions types found in the TOEFL® iBT, and are provided with practice of TOEFL® iBT reading, listening, speaking, and writing passages, conversations, lectures, and questions accessible to students of their level.

Basic Skills for the TOEFL® iBT enables students to build on both their language skills and their knowledge. The themes of the passages, lectures, and questions cover the topics often seen on the TOEFL® iBT. In addition, the independent topics, while taking place in a university setting, are also accessible to and understood by students preparing to enter university. The academic topics are also ones that native speakers study.

Students accumulate vocabulary over the series. Vocabulary learned at the beginning of the series will appear in passages and lectures later in the book, level, and series. Each level gets progressively harder. The vocabulary becomes more difficult, the number of vocabulary words to be learned increases, and the passages, conversations, and lectures get longer and increase in level. By the end of the series, students will know all 570 words on the standard Academic Word List (AWL) used by TESOL and have a solid foundation in and understanding of the TOEFL® iBT.

Not only will *Basic Skills for the TOEFL® iBT* start preparing students for the TOEFL® iBT, but it will also give students a well-rounded basis for either further academic study in English or further TOEFL® iBT study.

Introduction to the *Basic Skills for the TOEFL® iBT* Reading Book

This is the second reading book in the *Basic Skills for the TOEFL® iBT* series. Each unit has three passages relating to an overall topic. This introduces students to the topics they will see in the other three books—Listening, Speaking, and Writing—in level two. The passages in reading level two are longer and at a higher level, the questions are slightly more difficult, and there are more vocabulary words compared to reading level one.

Each unit is separated into four sections:

The following will outline the activities and aims of each section.

Getting Ready to Read

Key Vocabulary and TOEFL Vocabulary

Students begin by studying the vocabulary they will encounter in the following passage.
TOEFL® Vocabulary is the words that have been found to appear most often in TOEFL®
preparation materials or are Academic Word List (AWL) words. TOEFL® Vocabulary is the most
important words for the student to learn in order to build their vocabulary before further TOEFL®
study. **Key Vocabulary** is the other words that are important for the student to know in order
to understand the passage that will follow.

TOEFL Question Types

In this part, students will become familiar with:
- one or two of the question types that appear in the TOEFL® iBT reading section
- the common wording and the aims of the question types
- the strategy for correctly answering the question

Becoming familiar with the question types and how to answer them is important for the student,
as it will help them answer the questions appropriately. Level 2 builds on the strategies the student
learned in level 1.

Over the course of the book, all the reading question types will be covered.

Reading Passage

This is the first passage of the unit. It contains the vocabulary words learned on the previous
page and there should be few words that students are unfamiliar with. This helps students
become used to reading academic type passages but at a level they can understand. Students
are asked to number each paragraph of the passage with the correct main idea or purpose. This
enables them to become used to thinking about not only the passage in general but also what
the main idea is and how that main idea is developed and supported throughout the passage.

Note-taking

The next part is a summary. The blanks in the summary are facts that are important to the
understanding of the passage and are often also either Key or TOEFL® vocabulary. This helps
students visualize the organization of the passage and prepares students to take their own notes
during the real TOEFL® test.

TOEFL Questions

The next page gives students the opportunity to practice the question types they were introduced
to on the first page of the unit. There will be two of each question type, and they will be worded in
the same way as they are in the real TOEFL® test.

TOEFL Vocabulary Practice

Here, students find sentences that use the TOEFL® vocabulary that they learned at the beginning
of the section. This helps students practice the words in context.

Practice

Key Vocabulary and TOEFL Vocabulary

This is the Key vocabulary and TOEFL® vocabulary students will encounter in following passage. See previous section for a full explanation.

Reading Passage

Students read the second passage of the unit. The passage contains the vocabulary words learned above. The students should underline the key information in the passage. This is again to help the student to identify the main idea and how that main idea is developed and supported throughout the passage.

TOEFL Questions

This part gives students the opportunity to practice each question type they were introduced to in this unit and in the previous unit. These questions are worded in the same way as they are in the real TOEFL® test.

TOEFL Vocabulary Practice

The next part is sentences using the TOEFL® vocabulary the student learned at the beginning of the section. This helps students practice the words in context.

Test

The test contains the last and longest passage of the unit. It is similar to the real TOEFL® test but at an appropriate level for the student. It gives the student the opportunity to practice many question types at the same time. The test passage also uses many of the vocabulary words learned over the course of the unit.

Check-up

Question Type Review

These questions check the student understands the question type that was focused on throughout the unit.

Key Vocabulary Practice

This part is sentences using the Key vocabulary the student learned over the course of the unit. This helps students practice the words in context.

Reading Lesson Plan—50 minutes

Homework Check	5 min.	• Talk about any homework questions that the students did not understand. A combination of both teacher and peer explanations should be used.
Review	10 min.	• Review the strategies discussed in the previous unit and talk about other strategies students might have employed when they did homework. • Have a few students give an oral summary of the passages they read for homework. ✽ If the test section was not given as homework it should be completed here.
Main Lesson	30 min.	**Getting Ready to Read** **A. Learn the words** • Preview the vocabulary and have students read the words aloud. • Have students predict the topic of the first passage. • Talk about what parts of speech the words belong to. ✽ Vocabulary preview can also be done immediately before the first reading passage. **B. Learn the question types** • Introduce the TOEFL® question types. • Discuss strategies that can be applied to the question types. **C. Reading Passage** • Ask the students to read the passage within a given time (about 1 minute.) • Talk about the main points and the organization of the passage as a class. **D. Note-taking** • Have students fill in the summary in pairs or in groups. • Ask students to write a few questions using the target question types. **E. TOEFL Questions** • Ask students to do the questions. Then, as a class or in pairs, talk about the strategies the students used to answer the questions. • Ask students to make another question, using the target question type, by themselves or in pairs. They should then ask their peers to answer the question. **F. TOEFL Vocabulary Practice** • Ask students to complete the sentences and check their answers in pairs. **Practice** **A. Learn the words** • Preview the vocabulary and have students read the words aloud. • Talk about what parts of speech the words belong to.
Wrap-up	5 min.	• Check the strategies. • Give homework (the rest of the Practice section). ✽ The Test section and Check-up section can also be given as homework.

Teaching Tips

- In the real TOEFL® iBT Reading Section, each reading passage has the title above it, so students are encouraged to read the title first and predict what the passage is about.

- It is strongly recommended to teach the target vocabulary prior to reading.

- It is a good idea to have students make their own vocabulary list on their PC or notebook. Putting the words under thematic categories (categories of subjects) would be an effective way to study the words.

- It is important to emphasize understanding of the main idea of the passage. Students often read the passage without constructing the framework of the passage, which can make it difficult for them to understand the main points later.

- Note-taking practice needs to be done in class with the teacher's assistance in the beginning because not many students are familiar with note-taking. Gradually, have students take notes in groups, pairs, and then individually.

- At least one passage and the following questions should be done as an in-class activity; otherwise, students will not be able to understand the strategies and the new information.

- It is important to have the students read through the passage quickly (skim.)

- Timed-reading is an effective activity. Teachers can change the time limit as students' reading speed builds up. Do the same with the comprehension questions.

- Encourage students to do timed-reading even when they do their homework. It is a good idea for students to record their time on their individual books.

- Written and oral summary is recommended as the real TOEFL® iBT includes the summary question. In addition, it is a useful exercise to prepare for the speaking and writing sections.

- Students can use the definitions and synonyms in the vocabulary section when they summarize or paraphrase the passages.

- Use the test at the end of each unit as a progress check by recording the scores of the tests.

[01] History

Getting Ready to Read

A. Learn the words.

Key Vocabulary

writer	a person who writes books, stories, etc. as a profession
actor	a person who acts and performs in plays, movies, on TV, etc.
play	a story written to be performed and acted
live off	to depend on someone or something for money

TOEFL Vocabulary

divide	to separate into parts or groups
complete	to finish; to have all parts with nothing missing
record	a written document containing information or knowledge
period	an amount of time during which one main thing happens
retirement	the time that follows the end of somebody's working life

B. Learn the question types.

TOEFL Question Types

Vocabulary
The word X in the passage is closest in meaning to...
In stating X, the author means that...

- This question asks for the meaning of a word in the context of how it is used in the passage.
- The word is usually important for understanding part of the passage.
- When you choose your answer, ensure that the sentence still makes sense and that you haven't changed the meaning of the sentence.

Reference
The word X in the passage refers to...

- The referent (word being referred to) is not always the noun closest to the pronoun being asked about.
- The referent usually comes before the word being asked about.
- When you choose your answer, ensure that the sentence still makes sense and that you haven't changed the meaning of the sentence.

C. Read the passage. Number each paragraph with the correct main idea or purpose.

> 1. Information on the first part of Shakespeare's life
> 2. Information on the last part of Shakespeare's life
> 3. What the passage is about
> 4. Details on the first part of Shakespeare's life
> 5. Information on the second part of Shakespeare's life

William Shakespeare

___William Shakespeare lived in England from 1564 to 1616. He was one of the world's best writers. His life can be divided into three periods.

___The first twenty years of Shakespeare's life were spent in Stratford. During this time, he finished school and got married. He also became a father.

___There is not much information about the early part of Shakespeare's life. People often call this period of Shakespeare's life the "dark years." This is because no complete records of his life from this time can be found.

___The second part of Shakespeare's life was spent in the theater. He worked as an actor in London. He also wrote many plays. This period of his life lasted twenty-five years.

___The last part of Shakespeare's life was his retirement. He spent this time in Stratford. At this time, he lived off of the money he made from his earlier work.

D. Complete the summary notes by filling in the blanks.

> **Topic:**   William Shakespeare
> **Introduction:** Lived in England from 1564–_____.
>   One of world's _____.
>   Life divided into _____.
> **Period 1:**   First _____ years spent in Stratford.
>   Early part of his life often called the _____
>   because there are no _____ of it.
> **Period 2:**   Second part in the _____.
>   Worked as an _____ in London.
>   Wrote many _____ over twenty-five years.
> **Period 3:**   _____ spent in Stratford.
>   Lived off money from _____.

E. Choose the correct answers.

1. The word divided in the passage is closest in meaning to

(A) joined (B) separated

2. The word records in the passage is closest in meaning to

(A) documents (B) great achievements

3. The phrase this period in the passage refers to

(A) the second part of his life (B) 20 years

4. The phrase this time in the passage refers to

(A) the 1500s (B) the last part of his life

TOEFL Vocabulary Practice

F. Fill in the blanks with the correct words.

divided	period	completed	records	retirement

1. In the final _____ of his life, van Gogh painted around 900 paintings.

2. Banks keep _____ of all their customers.

3. Great Britain and France are _____ by a body of water called the English Channel.

4. Most people in North America begin their _____ when they turn sixty-five.

5. Michael Johnson _____ a 200-meter race in only 19.32 seconds!

Practice

A. Learn the words.

Key Vocabulary

cover	to be all over the surface of something
researcher	a person who searches for information
carving	a design that has been cut from a solid material such as wood or stone
priest	a spiritual leader in some Christian churches

TOEFL Vocabulary

empire	a group of countries ruled by one government
explore	to investigate unknown places
religious	believing in a set of beliefs based on a god or group of gods
royal	being or related to a king or queen
class	a social rank usually depending on family, wealth, or education

Reading Passage

B. Read the passage and underline the key information.

Machu Picchu

High in the mountains of Peru is an ancient, dead city. It is the city of Machu Picchu. This city has lasted for hundreds of years. However, nobody has lived there to take care of the buildings, structures, and streets.

When the city was first built, it had many strong buildings and streets. They were made out of stone. There was also a good road that led down from the mountains. It started at the top of the city and ended down at the main road below.

Incas lived in the city for a period of about one hundred years. Then, the Inca Empire fell. The people left Machu Picchu. Over time, plants grew to cover the streets and buildings. They covered most of the city. Many years later, in 1911, an American exploring the area found the city again.

Researchers have studied the old buildings and carvings of Machu Picchu. They have learned a lot about the city. For example, they have discovered that the builders divided the city into three parts. One part was for the common people. Another part was for priests and religious activities. The third part was for the royal family or high class people.

C. Choose the correct answers.

1. The word there in the passage refers to

(A) in the city   (B) on the street

2. The word main in the passage is closest in meaning to

(A) first   (B) important

3. According to the passage, where is Machu Picchu?

(A) At the bottom of a mountain
(B) On top of a mountain

4. According to the passage, all of the following were made of stone EXCEPT

(A) buildings   (B) roof tops   (C) streets

TOEFL Vocabulary Practice

D. Fill in the blanks with the correct words.

empire	explored	royal	class	religious

1. The Windsors are the _____ family of the United Kingdom.

2. The British ___emp_____ was very big and contained many countries.

3. Communists believe that people should not be divided by ____cl_____.

4. Many _____rel._____ people often go to a place of worship.

5. Marco Polo ____exp_____ many areas and wrote about his travels to China.

Read the passage.

The Development of Cities

People began farming over 10,000 years ago. Not everyone grew the same kinds of crops. Different areas of the world grew different crops. Farmers in the Middle East grew wheat, and farmers in China grew rice. Farming gave people more food. After farming, people began to raise animals. The first animals were raised for food. They included sheep, cows, goats, and pigs.

Farming helped people to stay in one place for a long period of time. This meant that people needed somewhere to live. They built stronger houses that would last for years. They also built places to store extra crops. They would eat some of the extra crops, but they would also trade or sell these crops for money. In this way, cities began to develop.

■ 1) Many people lived in the same city. This meant that not everyone needed to raise crops or animals. ■ 2) Some people could do special work. For example, workers would build houses, artists could make pots, arts, and crafts, and priests could do religious work. ■ 3) People learned to divide the jobs so that everyone in the city could benefit. ■ 4) This led to different classes of people.

Many people moved to cities. Some cities became very big. They covered large areas of land. They also became rich. These cities needed to remember how many people and crops there were. They needed to check what was traded or sold. Someone came up with the idea of writing this information down. With written records, things would not be forgotten. Ideas could be shared with other people. Writing allowed people in cities to complete many things. It helped them build structures like temples and palaces. It helped them to explore different ideas to make life better. This made cities even bigger. Countries and empires grew out of this system.

Choose the correct answers.

1. The word store in the passages is closest in meaning to
   (A) bury
   (B) collect
   (C) keep
   (D) purchase

2. According to the passage, all of the following were raised for food EXCEPT
   (A) cows
   (B) horses
   (C) pigs
   (D) sheep

3. Which of the following best expresses the essential information in the highlighted sentence? Incorrect answers change the meaning in important ways or leave out essential information.

> They would eat some of the extra crops, but they would also trade or sell these crops for money.

(A) People wanted to trade or sell the crops so that they could eat expensive food.
(B) Some people would eat the extra crops before they could be traded or sold.
(C) The extra crops might be eaten or sold.
(D) When people ate the extra crops, they would have to trade or sell other things.

4. Look at the four squares [■] that indicate where the following sentence could be added to the passage.

This led to different groups of people with specialized skills and abilities.

Where would the sentence best fit?

(A) Square 1   (B) Square 2
(C) Square 3   (D) Square 4

5. Which of the following can be inferred about early writing?

(A) It was not easy to learn.   (B) Not many kings could read it.
(C) It helped cities to improve.   (D) People used it to tell stories.

6. **Directions:** An introductory sentence for a brief summary of the passage is provided below. Complete the summary by selecting the THREE answer choices that express the most important ideas in the passage. Some sentences do not belong in the summary because they express ideas that are not presented in the passage or are minor ideas in the passage.

The development of certain things helped people go from living in small groups to building empires.

Answer choices

(A) Cities developed because people stayed in the same place and built strong structures to live in and store food in.
(B) Farmers kept some of their crops inside buildings, but they sold the rest.
(C) Living in cities made it possible for some people to do different kinds of work.
(D) Palaces were the most important structures in cities, so they were larger than temples or other buildings used by lots of people.
(E) Writing let people share ideas and remember things for a long time, both of which helped cities develop even more.

Check-up

A. Choose the correct answers.

1. When you come to a vocabulary question, you should
   (A) ensure your choice is an antonym of the word asked about
   (B) make sure your choice is found in the sentence before the word asked about
   (C) ensure your answer makes sense when substituted for the word asked about
   (D) make sure your answer sounds similar to the word asked about

2. What should you do when answering a reference question?
   (A) Choose the word closest to the pronoun being asked about.
   (B) Look closely at the words before the pronoun being asked about.
   (C) Select the word that is a synonym to the pronoun in question.
   (D) Eliminate all choices that occur before the pronoun in question.

Key Vocabulary Practice

B. Fill in the blanks with the correct words.

live off	play	carvings	priest
covered	researchers	writer	actor

1. If you need to see a _____, you can find one in a church.

2. Many people's favorite _____ is Angelina Jolie, but I don't like her films!

3. Many people invest money that they plan to _____ after they retire.

4. H.G. Wells is the _____ who wrote the science fiction book, *The Time Machine*.

5. One of the oldest stone _____ in the world is of a woman, and it may be 800,000 years old.

6. Almost seventy percent of the Earth is _____ by water.

7. I saw a _____ last week that had my favorite actor in it.

8. _____ are working hard to find a cure for cancer.

[02] Architecture

Getting Ready to Read

A. Learn the words.

Key Vocabulary

influential	having or exercising importance or influence
suit	to match well; to be appropriate for
hire	to give a job to someone
moral	conforming to what people consider right; just in behavior

TOEFL Vocabulary

architect	one who designs and supervises the construction of buildings
construction	the art, trade, or work of building
design	to create or to think of
define	to describe the meaning, nature, or basic qualities of something
tradition	a body of distinctive practices that is passed on from generation to generation

B. Learn the question types.

TOEFL Question Types

Factual Information
According to the paragraph, which of the following is true of X?
The author's description of X mentions which of the following?
According to the information in paragraph 1, why did X do Y?

- Eliminate answer choices you immediately recognize as incorrect.
- Scan the paragraph or section mentioned in the question for the relevant details.
- To ensure you fully understand the question, reread the whole section of the passage that is relevant to the fact asked about.

Negative Factual Information
According to the passage, which of the following is NOT true of X?
The author's description of X mentions all of the following EXCEPT...

- Scan the entire passage for the details mentioned in the answer choices.
- The correct answer choice is either not mentioned in the passage at all, or it contradicts a correct statement or detail that is mentioned.

C. Read the passage. Number each paragraph with the correct main idea or purpose.

> 1. Information on Frank Lloyd Wright's early career
> 2. Frank Lloyd Wright's contributions outside the United States
> 3. What the passage is about
> 4. Highlights of Frank Lloyd Wright's later career
> 5. Information on Frank Lloyd Wright's training

Frank Lloyd Wright

___Frank Lloyd Wright is one of the world's most influential architects. He is still the most famous American architect.

___Wright went to university in Wisconsin. While there, he trained with a construction company. He left after less than two years. He didn't graduate.

___In Chicago, he designed homes that suited the city. These homes defined his Prairie Period. However, after a while people in and around Chicago began to talk about his personal life. They thought he had no morals. He left the country because he couldn't get hired.

___He wrote a book in Europe. It had pictures of his houses. It encouraged several architectural traditions. Soon there were many books on his designs.

___When he returned to the US, he designed different buildings. He started the tradition of designing buildings that would suit the nature around them. His most famous building is Falling Water in Pennsylvania. It is built over a waterfall in a forest.

D. Complete the summary notes by filling in the blanks.

Topic: Frank Lloyd Wright

Introduction: Wright is a _____ American _____.

Training: Went to university in _____, but didn't _____.
Also trained with a _____ company.

Chicago: Designed homes that _____.
This time called his _____ Period.
No company would _____ him because they thought he had
no _____, so he _____.

Europe: Encouraged several _____ traditions by publishing a
_____ of pictures of his _____.

Return to US: Returned to the _____, and designed buildings to
_____ the world around them. _____
is the most famous of these.

E. Choose the correct answers.

1. According to the passage, which of the following is true of Frank Lloyd Wright?

(A) He built many buildings.   (B) People talked about his personal life.

2. According to the passage, the description of Falling Water mentions which of the following?

(A) The house was made of wood from nearby trees.

(B) Wright designed it to match its surroundings.

3. According to the passage, which of the following is NOT true of Frank Lloyd Wright's architectural training?

(A) He graduated from university.

(B) He learned how to design buildings by helping build them with a construction company.

4. According to the passage, which of the following was NOT a reason that Frank Lloyd Wright left the United States?

(A) He could not find any work.   (B) He wanted to publish a book.

TOEFL Vocabulary Practice

F. Fill in the blanks with the correct words.

designed	architect	construction	defined	traditions

1. The age we live in is _____ by a deep sense of uncertainty.

2. I.M. Pei is the _____ that created the Pyramids of the Louvre in 1989.

3. The Dalai Lama believes that all religious _____ carry the same message of love, compassion, and forgiveness.

4. Michelangelo _____ the uniforms worn by the Swiss guards at the Vatican.

5. Many people protested the _____ of the Eiffel Tower in 1887.

Practice

A. Learn the words.

Key Vocabulary

impractical	unwise to use or maintain
story	the set of rooms on the same level of a building
antenna	part of radio, television, and radar systems that directs incoming and outgoing radio waves
spire	a top part or point that tapers to a point at the top

TOEFL Vocabulary

civilization	an advanced state of intellectual, cultural, and material development in human society
constraint	something that restricts, limits, or regulates
debate	argument
element	a basic, essential part of something larger
technique	a method used in dealing with something/doing something

Reading Passage

B. Read the passage and underline the key information.

Tall Buildings

Many people see tall buildings as a sign of civilization. Yet, until the nineteenth century, it was rare to find a tall building. There were many constraints limiting the height of buildings. The taller the building, the stronger it has to be. Climbing the stairs made tall buildings impractical. It was also hard to get water up to the top.

Many things were needed to build tall buildings. Something strong enough to support tall buildings was needed. Steel was invented in the 1850s. Elevators meant people did not have to climb stairs. Water pumps could pump water up higher. Because of these things, the first sky scraper was built. It was in Chicago and it was only ten stories high. Until 1998, the tallest sky scrapers were in the US.

Now, the tallest sky scraper in the world is Taipei 101. It is 101 stories high. It is in Taiwan. There is some debate over its height. Some people wonder if elements such as antennas and spires should count. Taipei 101's spire is 60 feet high.

Building techniques are still improving. By 2012, there will be more than ten buildings taller than Taipei 101.

C. Choose the correct answer.

1. The word antennas in the passage is closest in meaning to
   (A) parts of a TV system   (B) foundations of a building

2. The word it in the passage refers to
   (A) the first sky scraper   (B) steel

3. According to the passage, where was the tallest building in the world in 1972?
   (A) Taiwan   (B) The United States

4. According to the passage, which of the following is NOT true of Taipei 101?
   (A) It is 200 stories high.   (B) Its spire is 60 feet high.

TOEFL Vocabulary Practice

D. Fill in the blanks with the correct words.

civilization	constraints	element	debate	technique

1. Great dancers aren't great because of their _____; they are great because of their passion.

2. Today, there is still great _____ over who really killed John F. Kennedy.

3. The most common _____ of racism is ignorance.

4. The Mayan _____ is the only American culture prior to the arrival of Christopher Columbus that had a fully developed written language, as well as spectacular art and architecture and sophisticated mathematics and astronomy.

5. Some people ignore all moral _____ in their pursuit of success.

Test

Read the passage.

Baroque Architecture

Baroque architecture was first constructed by European civilization in the early 1600s. The style was suited to the period. Leaders had gained more power. They were also very rich. They wanted buildings that showed this power and wealth. They wanted people to be amazed by their power.

Baroque architects trained in the classical Renaissance tradition. That tradition was defined by smooth lines and symmetry. Reason was the most important element of making anything extraordinary. The architects used these ideas, but emotion was also quite important. People in this period liked big buildings. They filled the insides of buildings with lots of art. Gardens and more art were on the outside. These buildings were imposing.

Many churches were built with these techniques during this period. The pope was very powerful. ■ 1) The churches had paintings on the ceiling and sculptures. ■ 2) The light let in by the windows was extraordinary. ■ 3) The construction workers hoped to make people believe in God. ■ 4) Today, people debate if this was successful or not.

All types of buildings were designed in this style: homes, town halls, banks, military buildings. The most well known are palaces. Kings believed their houses showed their right to rule. Kings were limited by very few constraints. The most famous Baroque palace is Versailles. As you walk inside, the rooms become more and more impressive. There are paintings on the ceiling. It has a theater and five chapels. When it was built, it was the biggest in Europe. Outside was one of the largest gardens in the world. The garden has a pretty, pretend town. It was very expensive. Many people believe that the kings of France spent too much on the palace. They think this expense was one of the reasons the people later removed the king.

Choose the correct answers.

1. The phrase these ideas in the passage refers to
   (A) Renaissance values
   (B) making buildings that were equal on each side
   (C) the paintings, sculpture, and other types of art
   (D) reason

2. Which of the following best expresses the essential information in the highlighted sentence? Incorrect answers change the meaning in important ways or leave out essential information.

   Kings believed their houses showed their right to rule.

   (A) The king believed people with Baroque buildings were show-offs.
   (B) Baroque buildings were expensive for kings.
   (C) Baroque buildings were intended as statements of the king's right to rule.
   (D) Wealthy people were expected to have their own Baroque building.

3. According to the passage, what are the most famous Baroque buildings?

(A) Palaces   (B) Churches

(C) Town halls   (D) Military buildings

4. The passage implies that _____ was least likely to build a Baroque building.

(A) a government   (B) the pope

(C) a teacher   (D) a monarchy

5. Look at the four squares [■] that indicate where the following sentence could be added to the passage.

Catholic churches tended to be more decorated than Protestant churches.

Where would the sentence best fit?

(A) Square 1   (B) Square 2

(C) Square 3   (D) Square 4

6. Directions: An introductory sentence for a brief summary of the passage is provided below. Complete the summary by selecting the THREE answer choices that express the most important ideas in the passage. Some sentences do not belong in the summary because they express ideas that are not presented in the passage or are minor ideas in the passage.

The Baroque style grew out of the political and artistic leanings of the 1600s in Europe.

Answer choices

(A) Baroque houses had elaborate gardens that served as a decoration for the building.

(B) From the rational classical Renaissance tradition, the Baroque developed a greater focus on arousing an emotional response from its audience.

(C) Very wealthy and powerful people built these great buildings to express their own greatness.

(D) Protestant Baroque churches had less decorative art than did Catholic churches.

(E) Popes and kings were the individuals for whom Baroque architecture embodied their right to rule.

Check-up

A. Choose the correct answers.

1. What should you do when you come to a factual information question?
   (A) Reread the entire passage for all of the relevant information.
   (B) Quickly reread the paragraph or section referred to in the question.
   (C) Choose all answers that are mentioned in the passage.
   (D) Select the choice that can best be inferred from information in the passage.

2. For negative factual information questions, you should
   (A) select an answer choice that is not mentioned in the passage
   (B) scan the passage for similar information to that in question
   (C) choose an answer choice that supports the main idea of the passage
   (D) look through the passage for the same information, worded differently

Key Vocabulary Practice

B. Fill in the blanks with the correct words.

influential	hire	suited	moral
stories	impractical	antenna	spire

1. These days, companies like to _____ people that have many different skills.

2. The _____ of the Salisbury Cathedral is the tallest in the United Kingdom.

3. Most hotels in North America and Europe that are over thirteen _____ high still do not have a thirteenth floor because the number thirteen is considered unlucky.

4. Right and wrong are often defined differently by individuals who each have a unique _____ code.

5. Evolution has ensured that most animals are _____ to their environments.

6. Albert Einstein was very _____ in the development of the atomic bomb.

7. Raising the Titanic to the surface has proved to be _____ because of the great expense involved.

8. There was no TV reception because the _____ had been damaged in the storm.

[03] Botany

Getting Ready to Read

A. Learn the words.

Key Vocabulary

development	the act of expanding, enlarging, or improving the quality of something
germinate	to cause to sprout or grow
nutrient	a source of nourishment, especially a nourishing ingredient in a food
pollinate	to transfer pollen onto the sexual organs of a flower, allowing the production of a seed

TOEFL Vocabulary

botany	the science or study of plants
investigation	a detailed inquiry or systematic examination
absorb	to soak up; to take in
establish	to bring about; to generate
distribute	to supply, deliver, or pass out

B. Learn the question type.

TOEFL Question Type

Sentence Simplification
Which of the following best expresses the essential information in the highlighted sentence? *Incorrect* answers change the meaning in important ways or leave out essential information.

- Look for synonyms of words in the highlighted passage in the answer choices.
- Ensure that the most important details of the highlighted passage are in the answer choice you choose, even if the sentence structure is different.
- Be careful to choose the answer choice that both contains the same important details and makes the same point as the highlighted passage.

C. Read the passage. Number each paragraph with the correct main idea or purpose.

1. The purpose of stems
2. The role of roots
3. Information on germination
4. Information on how plants produce their food
5. Information on plant reproduction

Plant Development

___ Botany is the investigation of plant development. Plants begin as seeds. When the seed germinates, it sends out a root, which grows downward.

___ Roots grow in soil or water. They get nutrients they require from the soil. Tiny hairs on the roots absorb water. Roots hold the plant in the ground and store food.

___ Then, the seed establishes a small stem. It will grow upward. The stem holds the leaves off the soil and protects them from the insects or animals that live there. The stem carries nutrients from the roots to the leaves.

___ Leaves are where the plant makes food. Using sunlight, green plants combine carbon dioxide and water to make sugar and oxygen. We eat plants for this sugar energy.

___ Most plants produce seeds. To produce seeds, the plants must be pollinated. Flowers tend to be colorful and smell nice to attract pollinators. The pollinators distribute the pollen.

Note-taking

D. Complete the summary notes by filling in the blanks.

Topic: Plant Development
Introduction: Study of plant development called _____.
              Plants begin as _____.
              _____ grow downward from seeds.
Roots: Roots grow in _____.
              They provide plants with _____ and water.
              They hold plant in the _____.
Stem: Stems develop upward from _____.
              They keep plant leaves away from some _____.
              They bring nutrients from the _____ to the _____.
Leaves: Leaves make _____ from sunlight, CO_2, and water.
              The food is _____ and _____.
Seeds: Plants must be _____ to make seeds.
              Colorful, nice-smelling _____ attract pollinators to distribute
              _____.

E. Choose the correct answers.

1. Which of the following best expresses the essential information in the highlighted sentence? Incorrect answers change the meaning in important ways or leave out essential information.

When the seed germinates, it sends out a root, which grows downward.

(A) A vertical shoot is the first thing that grows from a germinating seed.
(B) A seed is the first thing that grows from a successful root.

2. Which of the following best expresses the essential information in the highlighted sentence? Incorrect answers change the meaning in important ways or leave out essential information.

The stem holds the leaves off the soil and protects them from the insects or animals that live there.

(A) Stems protect the important part of a plant from all animals.
(B) The stem develops to protect the leaves of a plant.

TOEFL Vocabulary Practice

F. Fill in the blanks with the correct words.

botany	investigation	established	distributed	absorbs

1. Police typically carry out an _____ in order to find out who committed a crime.

2. Dr. William Hillebrand, a _____ expert, was the first to record and study Hawaii's plant life in detail.

3. During World War II, the Allies _____ pamphlets to the Germans to damage their morale.

4. A special skin on the F-117 stealth fighter _____ radar waves, making it invisible to radar.

5. In 1910, Andrew Carnegie _____ the Endowment for International Peace in an effort to prevent future wars.

Practice

A. Learn the words.

Key Vocabulary

corpse	a dead body
nickname	an often-humorous invented name for someone or something
deforestation	the act of removing trees from a forest
cultivation	the act of growing or tending a plant or crop

TOEFL Vocabulary

distinct	easily perceived by the senses of intellect; clear
emerge	to come into existence
region	a portion of the Earth's surface
obtain	to get; to acquire
maintenance	the work of keeping something in proper condition

Reading Passage

B. Read the passage and underline the key information.

The Corpse Flower

The corpse flower received its nickname because of its distinct smell. The flower smells like a dead body. In fact, natives of Sumatra, Indonesia, thought it ate meat. They would destroy the flower so it could not eat them. The smell is so strong that humans can smell it a half mile away. The smell attracts the insects that pollinate the flower.

The flower looks impressive. It is a big plant. The flower head can grow up to ten feet tall. The flower emerges from a giant root that can weigh nearly 200 pounds. When it is not blooming, it has a big leaf that grows up to twenty feet tall.

It likes the shade, warmth, and rich, moist soil of the western Sumatra region. Unfortunately, the plant is becoming very rare. Deforestation is destroying the places where it grows. People who like to obtain rare flowers dig it up. There may be none left in the wild soon.

There are few corpse flowers outside of Sumatra. They were first sent to Europe in 1878. Sadly, it rarely flowers outside of Sumatra. With careful maintenance, however, botanists can sometimes help it to bloom outside the wild. It is much smaller in cultivation.

C. Choose the correct answers.

1. Which of the following best expresses the essential information in the highlighted sentence? Incorrect answers change the meaning in important ways or leave out essential information.

   They would destroy the flower so it could not eat them.

   (A) The natives killed the corpse flower because it was a carnivore.
   (B) The natives killed the corpse flower because they thought it ate people.

2. According to the passage, which of the following climate conditions are required for the corpse flower to grow?
   (A) Warmth, direct sunlight, and rain
   (B) Hot weather, shade, and lots of rain

3. According to the passage, which of the following is NOT one of the reasons for the rarity of the corpse flower?
   (A) Animal activity   (B) Human activity

TOEFL Vocabulary Practice

D. Fill in the blanks with the correct words.

distinct	emerged	regions	obtained	maintenance

1. In the sixteenth century, Spain _____ most of its gold from the New World.

2. Hardware _____ requires the testing and cleaning of equipment.

3. The Nazi movement in Germany _____ after the Great War.

4. The mountainous _____ of Canada are known for their ski resorts.

5. Cockney is a _____ dialect of English spoken in East London.

Read the passage.

Plant Survival

One area of botany studies how plants adapt to different regions. An investigation of desert plants is a perfect example of this. We often imagine that no plants live in the desert. However, the desert is home to many species of plant life. Some plants survive because of physical adaptations; others adjust their behavior.

Plants have developed two different ways to survive in the desert. The first type developed long roots. These roots are distributed underground. Their roots allow them to obtain nutrients and water far below ground. An example of this type is the mesquite tree. ■ 1) Its roots grow up to eighty feet deep. ■ 2) They are longer than the roots of other desert plants. ■ 3) Mesquite trees can live for more than 200 years. ■ 4) The other type of plant developed special ways to store and save water. The most famous one is the cactus. It has no leaves because plants lose water through their leaves. It has wide shallow roots so it can quickly obtain lots of rain water. Its stem can absorb a lot of water. Its spines are good for providing shade. Its waxy skin seals in moisture. It can survive for years without much water. This makes cacti popular plants because they require almost no maintenance.

Other plants adjust their behavior to the desert. Some flowers only grow leaves when it is wet. One only emerges only after rainfall. When it is dry, the plant loses its leaves. When it rains, it establishes them again. This plant blooms up to five times per year.

Some plants are distinct because they are very short-lived. The desert sand verbena grows seeds in only a few weeks after a heavy rain. It has very hardy seeds. Then it dies. Its seeds wait until the next rain. They can emerge, even after three years.

Choose the correct answers.

1. Which of the following can be inferred about mesquite trees?

(A) It would be easy to get water if you found a mesquite tree.
(B) They would die if there was no rain.
(C) They are bigger than other desert plants.
(D) They are hard to kill.

2. The word adapt in the passage is closest in meaning to

(A) change   (B) grow
(C) interbreed   (D) adjust

3. Look at the four squares [■] that indicate where the following sentence could be added to the passage.

If you are lost in the desert you can even survive by eating the beans that grow on it.

Where would the sentence best fit?

(A) Square 1

(B) Square 2

(C) Square 3

(D) Square 4

4. Which of the following best expresses the essential information in the highlighted sentence? Incorrect answers change the meaning in important ways or leave out essential information.

The other type of plant developed special ways to store and save water.

(A) One way for a plant to survive in the desert is to grow long roots.

(B) Physical adaptation has allowed other types of plant to store and save water in the desert.

(C) Plants must act in ways that do not waste water.

(D) Plants must develop large leaves to collect water.

5. According to the passage, which of the following is NOT a plant adaptation to desert regions?

(A) Long roots

(B) Skin that holds in water

(C) Few leaves

(D) Extra flowers

6. **Directions:** An introductory sentence for a brief summary of the passage is provided below. Complete the summary by selecting the THREE answer choices that express the most important ideas in the passage. Some sentences do not belong in the summary because they express ideas that are not presented in the passage or are minor ideas in the passage.

Plants have developed a number of successful ways of surviving in the desert.

Answer choices

(A) Some plants modify the way they grow in order to take better advantage of periods of rain.

(B) Although they do not live very long, annuals are ideally suited to the desert.

(C) Cacti are excellent plants to cultivate because they require little water.

(D) Some plants change physically, in order to better collect and conserve water.

(E) The variety of different ways that plants have adapted to the desert is as broad as the many different plants the desert supports.

Check-up

A. Choose the correct answer.

1. What should you do when you come to a sentence simplification question?
   (A) Choose the answer that is longer than the highlighted passage.
   (B) Look for antonyms of words in the highlighted passage in the answer choices.
   (C) Look for synonyms of words in the highlighted passage in the answer choices.
   (D) Select the answer that contradicts the important points in the highlighted passage.

2. When you come to a sentence simplification question, you should
   (A) look for answer choices with the same sentence structure as the highlighted passage
   (B) select the answer that contains the most important details of the highlighted passage
   (C) scan the answer choices for the sentence that uses the same words as the highlighted passage
   (D) choose the answer that leaves out the most important details of the highlighted passage

Key Vocabulary Practice

B. Fill in the blanks with the correct words.

development	germinate	nutrients	pollinate
nickname	deforestation	cultivation	corpse

1. A doctor can determine the cause of death by examining the _____.

2. _____, like vitamins, are essential for good health.

3. Most seeds will _____ if they are given water and plenty of sunshine.

4. "Philly" is a _____ for the city of Philadelphia in the United States.

5. Indoor botanical gardens are interested in the _____ of plants from all over the world.

6. The _____ of the tropics is causing loss of habitat for many plants and animals.

7. The _____ of the oil industry in the Middle East was started by Great Britain.

8. Bats are important because they _____ some tropical flowers in the rainforest.

[04] Chemistry

Getting Ready to Read

A. Learn the words.

Key Vocabulary

grain	a tiny single piece
positive charge	one of two electric properties of matter
negative charge	one of two electric properties of matter
atomic	having to do with atoms

TOEFL Vocabulary

approximately	about; close to, but not exact
atom	the smallest part of an element
foundation	the basis of something
specify	to state something in detail or explicitly
dense	packed together tightly

B. Learn the question types.

TOEFL Question Types

Inference

What probably occurred after X?

Which of the following can be inferred from paragraph A about X?

- Scan the passage or paragraph specified for the information given in the question.
- Eliminate answer choices that are inaccurate or not mentioned in the passage.
- Ensure that your answer choice is logically supported by details in the passage.

Rhetorical Purpose

Why does the author compare X to Y?

Why does the author use the word X in discussing Y?

The author discusses X in paragraph 2 in order to...

- Familiarize yourself with the meanings of various purpose vocabulary used in these questions, such as the following: argue, classify, compare, contrast, criticize, emphasize, illustrate, persuade, summarize, etc.
- Carefully read for connections between the points raised in the question.
- Choose the answer that provides the most logical explanation for the author's writing.

C. Read the passage. Number each paragraph with the correct main idea or purpose.

> 1. What the proton does
> 2. What each atom is made of
> 3. Introduction to how small atoms are
> 4. What an atom looks like
> 5. What atoms do

The Atom

___Imagine a grain of sand. It is very small. Now imagine that each grain of sand contains approximately 78,000,000,000,000,000,000 atoms.

___Atoms are the foundation of everything in the world. Your heart, your mother's gold ring, and even this book are all made from atoms.

___Each single atom is made up of three parts—protons, neutrons, and electrons. Protons are positively charged, neutrons have no charge, and electrons are negatively charged.

___The number of protons that an atom has specifies what an atom is. This number of protons is called the atomic number. For example, an atom with an atomic number of seventy-nine is gold. One with eight is oxygen.

___The structure of an atom is very basic. The core or nucleus of an atom consists of protons and neutrons. The core is very dense. Electrons orbit around the core like planets around the Sun.

D. Complete the summary notes by filling in the blanks.

Topic:	The Atom
Size:	Grain of sand has _____ atoms.
Importance:	Atoms are _____ of all things.
Parts:	Atom has _____ parts.
	_____ have a positive charge.
	_____ have a neutral charge.
	_____ have a negative charge.
Identification:	The number of _____ specifies what an atom is.
	Number of protons is called the _____.
Core:	The core has _____ and _____.
	Electrons _____ around core.

E. Choose the correct answers.

1. Which of the following can be inferred from paragraph 1?

   (A) Atoms are very small.
   (B) Atoms are really heavy.

2. Which of the following can be inferred from paragraph 4?

   (A) Even one proton can make a big difference to how an atom acts.
   (B) Gold is more expensive than oxygen because it has more protons.

3. Why did the author include the phrase like planets around the Sun?

   (A) He wanted to show the reader how electrons in an atom move.
   (B) He wanted to show that planets are also made of atoms.

4. Why did the author state that each grain of sand contains approximately 78,000,000,000,000,000,000 atoms?

   (A) To discuss how many grains of sand there are on the beach
   (B) To make sure the reader understands the size being discussed

TOEFL Vocabulary Practice

F. Fill in the blanks with the correct words.

atom	dense	foundation	approximately	specifies

1. Many Asian cities have very _____ populations because there are so many people and so little space.

2. The discovery of the _____ ultimately led to the development of nuclear weapons.

3. There are _____ three hundred million people living in America.

4. The owner's guide always _____ how you should care for your computer.

5. Democracy is the _____ of the American government system.

Practice

A. Learn the words.

Key Vocabulary

laboratory	a place to do scientific research
dissolve	to disappear or absorb into water
weak	not strong; lacking in power
bubble	a thin ball of air

TOEFL Vocabulary

associate	to connect with someone or something else
invisible	unable to be seen
reaction	a response to something happening
occur	to happen; to take place
react	to change chemically

Reading Passage

B. Read the passage and underline the key information.

Chemistry and Soda

Normally when people think of chemistry, they think of a scientist in a laboratory. We think of dangerous things being made that can hurt people. We don't normally associate chemistry with food or drinks.

Have you ever wondered why orange soda is sweet, has bubbles, and tastes like oranges? The answer to these questions lies in chemistry.

Soda is sweet because it is made from sugar and water. However, when you finish a can, you never see any white sugar. This is because the sugar dissolves into the water and becomes invisible.

Most sodas contain a weak acid. Some people have tried to show that this acid is dangerous. If you put a rusty nail in soda, the acid in the soda will react with the rust on the nail. This reaction will make the rust disappear. People think that this means the acid is very strong and that it can hurt your stomach. But it is unlikely this reaction will occur, as the acid is very weak.

Finally, the soda gets its orange taste from chemistry. This happens because scientists make formulas. They then put these in the soda. This formula then reacts with our tongue and nose. It makes us taste oranges.

C. Choose the correct answers.

1. Why did the author include the first paragraph?

(A) To show you that chemistry has many more uses than you might think

(B) To tell you that he or she is a scientist

2. What can be inferred about the taste of orange soda?

(A) Chemistry makes oranges.

(B) There are no actual oranges in orange soda.

3. Which of the following best expresses the essential information in the highlighted sentence? Incorrect answers change the meaning in important ways or leave out essential information.

Soda is sweet because it is made from sugar and water.

(A) The taste of soda comes from a combination of sugar and water.

(B) The acid in the soda makes it very sweet.

TOEFL Vocabulary Practice

D. Fill in the blanks with the correct words.

associated	invisible	reaction	react	occur

1. Children can make _____ ink by mixing baking soda and water.

2. Some chemicals can _____ violently when mixed, so you must be careful and always listen to your teacher.

3. Solar eclipses only _____ every eighteen months or so.

4. Einstein will forever be _____ with his famous equation, $E=MC^2$.

5. The director's goal is to get a positive _____ from the audience to his or her movie.

Test

Read the passage.

Chemistry Experiments

Did you know that chemistry is the foundation of all life? Have you ever wanted to study chemistry but didn't have a laboratory to do it in? The following experiments are fun and easy. They can also all be done from your home!

The first test that you can do from your home involves acids. This test will help you to specify which liquids in your house are acids or not. This is very easy. First, buy some red cabbage. Then put some of the liquid on the cabbage. If the cabbage stays red, the acid is very strong. If the cabbage changes to a different color, like purple or violet, then the liquid is a weak acid.

Another much more exciting test uses a bottle of diet soda, and a pack of Mentos. First, you should go outside. Then, simply put the candy into the bottle. The candy will react with the soda and bubbles will form. Soon the soda will start to shoot out of the bottle. Sometimes, the spray shoots approximately two meters in the air. When the candy has dissolved, the spray will stop. This reaction occurs because of the formulas of the soda and candy. So be careful the next time you eat candy and soda. You might get everyone around you really messy!

■ 1) There are some fun, easy, and safe ways for you to learn about chemistry. ■ 2) It is always important to have adults helping you. ■ 3) Chemistry is a lot of fun. But it can also be very dangerous. It is important to always listen to your teacher when in the laboratory. One small mistake can hurt a lot of people. ■ 4) It is a good idea to always associate chemistry with safety.

Choose the correct answers.

1. The word experiments in the passage is closest in meaning to

    (A) tests   (B) chemistry

    (C) acid   (D) shoot

2. According to the passage, all of the following things happen when candy is put in diet soda EXCEPT

    (A) bubbles form
    (B) soda shoots into the air
    (C) everything around gets wet
    (D) the bottle explodes

3. Which of the following best expresses the essential information in the highlighted sentence? Incorrect answers change the meaning in important ways or leave out essential information.

Sometimes, the spray shoots approximately two meters in the air.

(A) Sometimes it doesn't spray.
(B) The soda can spray two meters straight up and sometimes higher.
(C) The soda can spray two meters in the air but usually it is less.
(D) The candy gets shot almost two meters in the air.

4. Look at the four squares [■] that indicate where the following sentence could be added to the passage.

Chemistry can be great fun, but make sure to be safe while doing it.

Where would the sentence best fit?

(A) Square 1
(B) Square 2
(C) Square 3
(D) Square 4

5. Which of the following can be inferred when a cabbage changes color after a liquid is put on it?

(A) The cabbage is magic.
(B) The liquid shows invisible colors.
(C) A reaction occurs that makes the colors change.
(D) The cabbage doesn't like the liquid put on it.

6. **Directions:** An introductory sentence for a brief summary of the passage is provided below. Complete the summary by selecting the THREE answer choices that express the most important ideas in the passage. Some sentences do not belong in the summary because they express ideas that are not presented in the passage or are minor ideas in the passage.

Chemistry can be fun, but it is important to follow instructions.

Answer choices

(A) If red cabbage turns blue, it means that the liquid is a base.
(B) You should always be careful when doing chemistry.
(C) Chemistry can make strange things happen—like soda shoot into the air, and cabbage change colors.
(D) You should be careful when putting candy and soda into your mouth at the same time.
(E) There are many easy experiments that can be done from your home.

Check-up

A. Choose the correct answers.

1. What should you do when you come to an inference question?

   (A) Choose the answer choice with the specific information given in the question.
   (B) Choose the answer choice that contradicts the information given in the passage.
   (C) Ensure your answer choice is logically supported by details in the passage.
   (D) Ensure your answer choice best expresses the main idea of the passage.

2. When you come to a rhetorical purpose question, you should

   (A) carefully read for connections between the points raised in the question
   (B) choose the answer choice that contains a synonym for the word mentioned in the question
   (C) scan the passage for synonyms of the word mentioned in the question
   (D) select the answer choice that best suggests what will occur next

Key Vocabulary Practice

B. Fill in the blanks with the correct words.

atomic	grains	positive charge	negative charge
dissolve	laboratories	bubbles	weak

1. The proton is the particle of the atom that carries a _____.

2. People often like to blow _____ with their chewing gum.

3. Hourglasses are timing devices that consist of _____ of sand falling from one glass chamber into another.

4. Today's modern _____ are far more advanced than anything Isaac Newton could have imagined.

5. The Manhattan Project was the code name of the project that developed the _____ bomb.

6. Citric acid is a _____ acid that occurs naturally in lemons and other citrus fruits.

7. If you _____ salt into water, the water will boil faster.

8. The electron is the particle of the atom that carries a _____.

[05] Business

Getting Ready to Read

A. Learn the words.

Key Vocabulary

boost	to help or increase
off-season	a time of year during which sales are down
during	over a period of time
make sense	to be reasonable

TOEFL Vocabulary

seasonal	occurring during certain seasons or times of year
expense	a cost
employ	to pay workers to do a particular job
typical	representative; normal; average
staff	a group of workers

B. Learn the question type.

TOEFL Question Type

Insert Text

Look at the four squares [■] that indicate where the following sentence could be added to the passage.

[You will see a sentence in bold.]

Where would the sentence best fit?

- Try inserting the sentence into each place marked by a square [■], and eliminate any that are obviously incorrect.
- Look for logical connections in content between the sentence given and the sentences before and after each square.
- Look for structural connections, like pronouns and referents, parallel grammatical structure, or transitional words and phrases.
- Choose the position that makes the most logical and structural sense with the rest of the passage.

C. Read the passage. Number each paragraph with the correct main idea or purpose.

1. Information about seasonal businesses that close for part of the year
2. Information about seasonal businesses that stay open all year
3. Definition of seasonal business
4. Information about workers at seasonal businesses

Seasonal Businesses

___Some businesses only make money at certain times of the year. They are called seasonal businesses.

___Some of these businesses stay open all year. They make most of their money in one season. So, they try to boost sales in the off-season. ■ **1)** One way to do this is to sell at low prices. ■ **2)** That is why skis are cheaper in July. ■ **3)** They are hard to sell then. ■ **4)**

___Others close during the off-season. It does not make sense to stay open all year. They cannot make money during the off-season. For example, ski slopes cannot open during the summer months. There is no snow at this time, so it is not worth the expense to stay open. This is because they would still have to pay staff but not sell anything.

___ ■ **5)** Summer businesses often employ students. ■ **6)** This is because the typical student does not study in the summer. ■ **7)** It is more difficult to find staff for winter businesses. ■ **8)**

D. Complete the summary notes by filling in the blanks.

Topic: Seasonal Businesses
Introduction: Makes _____ at certain times of year.
All year: Some stay _____ all year.
Make most money in one _____.
Try to _____ sales in _____.
Off season: Some close _____ off-season.
Doesn't _____ to stay open.
Not worth the _____.
Staff: Summer businesses—_____ students.
Winter businesses—hard to find _____.

E. Choose the correct answers.

1. Look at the four squares [■] that indicate where the following sentence could be added to the passage.

They are expensive in the winter because demand is high.

Where would the sentence best fit?

(A) Square 1   (B) Square 2
(C) Square 3   (D) Square 4

2. Look at the four squares [■] that indicate where the following sentence could be added to the passage.

He or she takes the opportunity to earn extra money.

Where would the sentence best fit?

(A) Square 5   (B) Square 6
(C) Square 7   (D) Square 8

TOEFL Vocabulary Practice

F. Fill in the blanks with the correct words.

seasonal	expenses	employ	typical	staff

1. The area hopes to attract new businesses that will _____ local residents.

2. This building is _____ of the Victorian era.

3. She had enough money to pay tuition, but not enough to cover her living _____.

4. The cafeteria _____ is going on strike. They are demanding better pay and benefits.

5. He is a fisherman. That's _____ work, so he does odd jobs to get by in the winter months.

Practice

A. Learn the words.

Key Vocabulary

stick	to adhere; to follow strictly
lucky	fortunate
early on	in the beginning; in the first part of an event
goods	products; tangible items that are bought and sold

TOEFL Vocabulary

finances	monetary resources
budget	a plan for managing money
competitor	a firm that sells a similar product or service, who competes for market share
persuade	to convince
alternatively	or; as another choice

Reading Passage

B. Read the passage and underline the key information.

Business Finance

When you open a business, you want to make money. ■ 1) Therefore, how you manage your finances is important. ■ 2)

Creating a budget can be difficult. Sticking to that budget is even harder. You need to spend less than you make. Sometimes you won't be able to do this. ■ 3) For example, you have to pay your staff. ■ 4) Even if the business doesn't make any money, staff have to be paid. If you don't have enough funds to pay staff, you will go into debt.

You might be lucky. You might earn a profit early on. If you do, do not spend it on yourself. Put it back into the business. It takes money to make money. Therefore, you want to use the profits. It will help you make a better business. You might be able to hire more staff. You might be able to make more goods. All this may help you make more money.

How much you sell your goods or services for is also important. You should watch what your competitors charge. You have to persuade people to choose you. You might do this by selling at a lower price. Alternatively, you might charge more. Then you can provide better goods or services.

C. Choose the correct answers.

1. Look at the four squares [■] that indicate where the following sentence could be added to the passage.

You need to keep track of everything and spend money wisely.

Where would the sentence best fit?

(A) Square 1　　　　　　　　　　(B) Square 2
(C) Square 3　　　　　　　　　　(D) Square 4

2. Which of the following can be inferred about businesses?

(A) They fail if owners don't follow a proper budget.
(B) They succeed only if owners don't draw a salary.

3. Why does the author mention competitors?

(A) To emphasize the importance of paying staff
(B) To suggest a tool for setting prices

TOEFL Vocabulary Practice

D. Fill in the blanks with the correct words.

| finances | budget | competitor | persuade | alternatively |

1. He needs to learn to live within a _____ and stop spending so recklessly.

2. She had to cut her prices when a _____ began offering the same service for half the price.

3. The boy tried to _____ his parents to buy him a car, but they told him to get a job and save up for one.

4. You can choose to write a research paper or, _____, you can do volunteer work and give a class presentation about your experience.

5. Now, university in America is so expensive that many students do not have the _____ to go.

Test

Read the passage.

Jibbitz

Every business starts out as an idea. You can go to university to learn about business. Alternatively, you could start a business doing something that you really enjoy.

Sheri was a typical stay-at-home mom. She had three daughters. They all loved to do arts and crafts. One day, Sheri put a fake flower in the hole of one of her kid's "Crocs." Crocs are a popular rubber shoe. Her kids thought that it looked cute. They persuaded their mom to make more.

Sheri and her kids decorated their Crocs. They called them "Jibbitz." Then the girls wore them to school. Soon, all of their friends wanted some decorations for their shoes, too. Sheri and her husband, Rich, saw a good business opportunity. Many people already owned Crocs. ■ **1)** Decorations would make them more fun. They were also lucky because no one else was doing it. That means that they had no competitors. They looked at their finances and made a budget. They could see that the starting expenses would be cheap. They just had to buy materials. During this time, all the work was done by hand. They did not need a factory. They didn't need to employ any staff. They could do the work themselves. ■ **2)**

Jibbitz became very popular early on. They could not keep up with demand. So, they bought a factory and employed some staff. ■ **3)** In time, the company that makes Crocs bought the business from them. Sheri and Rich still run the business. They understand that Crocs may not always be popular. ■ **4)** That is why they come up with new ideas all the time. If they cannot sell Jibbitz for Crocs, they can design other goods. They are working on other things like hats and belts. That way, when Crocs go out of style, they will still be in business.

Choose the correct answers.

1. Which of the following best expresses the essential information in the highlighted sentence? Incorrect answers change the meaning in important ways or leave out essential information.

   Alternatively, you could start a business doing something that you really enjoy.

   (A) Optionally, you could study something you are interested in.
   (B) Consequently, you can have more time for your hobbies
   (C) Preferably you could try to enjoy your business.
   (D) Or you could create a business out of a hobby.

2. The word run in paragraph 4 is closest in meaning to
   (A) manage   (B) sprint
   (C) range   (D) endure

3. According to the passage, which of the following is NOT true of Sheri and Rich's business?

(A) It had no competition.
(B) Starting costs were low.
(C) The children did all the work.
(D) It was sold.

4. Look at the four squares [■] that indicate where the following sentence could be added to the passage.

So, they got to work in their basement.

Where would the sentence best fit?

(A) Square 1
(C) Square 3

(B) Square 2
(D) Square 4

5. What can be inferred from the passage about the Jibbitz business?

(A) It made a lot of money.
(B) It could not compete with Crocs.
(C) It will go out of business when the fad passes.
(D) It will always be the industry standard.

6. **Directions:** An introductory sentence for a brief summary of the passage is provided below. Complete the summary by selecting the THREE answer choices that express the most important ideas in the passage. Some sentences do not belong in the summary because they express ideas that are not presented in the passage or are minor ideas in the passage.

Some very successful businesses begin as ideas that come from hobbies.

Answer choices

(A) Sheri came up with her idea to make decorations for Crocs while doing arts and crafts with her daughters.
(B) Sheri's daughter inspired the idea by putting a flower in her favorite Crocs.
(C) Her daughters created demand by wearing them to school.
(D) It cost little to start and soon the business was a huge success.
(E) Now the Crocs company is trying to buy the company, but Sheri and Rich refuse to sell.

Check-up

A. Choose the correct answer.

1. What should you do when you come to an insert text question?
   (A) Look for details in the sentence given that repeat in the sentence after each square.
   (B) Look for the essential details from the sentence given in the sentence before each square.
   (C) Eliminate positions with structural connections to the sentences before and after it.
   (D) Choose the position that makes the most logical and structural sense with the rest of the passage.

Key Vocabulary Practice

B. Fill in the blanks with the correct words.

boost	off-season	during	make sense
stick	luck	early on	goods

1. Though summer is the _____ for ski resorts, many people still like to visit and spend time in the mountains.

2. When you make a promise to someone, you should try to _____ to it.

3. It doesn't _____ to leave the windows open if the air conditioner is on.

4. It takes more than _____ to win at poker. You also need skill.

5. The student was punished for talking _____ class.

6. When you return to your home country, you sometimes have to pay a tax on _____ that you purchased while you were on vacation.

7. An event, such as the World Cup or the Olympics, can be a big _____ to the local economy.

8. Even _____ in his career, basketball coaches could tell that Michael Jordan would be a great player.

[06] Geology

Getting Ready to Read

A. Learn the words.

Key Vocabulary

mineral	a type of matter that is uniform and is not from a plant or animal
composition	what something is made of
texture	the feel of a surface or fabric
landform	a feature of the Earth's surface

TOEFL Vocabulary

geology	the study of the Earth and its structures and processes
physical	dealing with material things
aspect	a feature, element, or characteristic
consistent	the same throughout
identify	to recognize as being a certain thing

B. Learn the question types.

TOEFL Question Type

Summary

An introductory sentence for a brief summary of the passage is provided below. Complete the summary by selecting the THREE answer choices that express the most important ideas in the passage. Some sentences do not belong in the summary because they express ideas that are not presented in the passage or are minor ideas in the passage. This question is worth two points.

This will be a correct summary sentence written in bold.

There will be three spaces for correct answers.
• Return to the passage and scan for the most important points.
• Eliminate answer choices that include irrelevant points or points not mentioned in the passage.
• Move the answer choices that include those most important points into the three spaces for correct answers.
• One point is awarded for getting two of three correct, so fill in all spaces even if you are not certain.

C. **Read the passage. Number each paragraph with the correct main idea or purpose.**

> 1. Information on the make-up of the Earth
> 2. Definition of geology
> 3. Example of something we can learn from geology
> 4. Information on what geologists do
> 5. Information about rocks

Geology

___Geology studies the physical aspects of the Earth. It looks at the materials that make up the Earth. It also looks at what happens to these materials over time.

___The Earth is made up of rocks, which are made up of minerals. Minerals are solids with a consistent composition. They are not made up of a mixture of things.

___There are three different types of rock. They have different textures and are made up of different minerals. Rocks can change from one type to another as they go through the rock cycle.

___Geologists identify rocks to learn about the history of the Earth. They can look at changes in landforms and figure out what happened in the past.

___We can learn about living things from the past by looking at rocks. Sometimes, when a plant or animal dies, it leaves a mark in the rock. This is called a fossil.

Note-taking

D. **Complete the summary notes by filling in the blanks.**

Topic:	Geology
Introduction:	Studies _____ of the Earth.
	Looks at _____ and what happens to them.
Composition:	Earth made of _____.
	Rocks made of _____.
	Minerals have _____.
Types of rocks:	_____ types of rock.
	Different _____ and _____.
	Change via the rock _____.
Study rocks to:	Geologists _____ rocks to learn history.
	Look at changes in _____.
Learn:	Learn about living things by looking at _____.

E. Choose the correct answers.

1. Directions: An introductory sentence for a brief summary of the passage is provided below. Complete the summary by selecting the THREE answer choices that express the most important ideas in the passage. Some sentences do not belong in the summary because they express ideas that are not presented in the passage or are minor ideas in the passage.

Geology is the study of the Earth, its composition, and what happens to it.

Answer Choices

(A) Rocks, which consist of minerals, make up the Earth.
(B) There are three types of rocks that change form via the rock cycle.
(C) Salt is the most plentiful mineral on Earth.
(D) We can learn about the history of the land and of living things by looking at rocks.
(E) Geologists are mainly interested in fossils.

TOEFL Vocabulary Practice

F. Fill in the blanks with the correct words.

geology	physical	aspect	consistent	identify

1. The artist discussed every _____ of her work from subject to color.

2. It is a good idea to make sure you know how to _____ poison ivy so you can avoid it.

3. I don't like psychology. I'm more interested in the _____ sciences.

4. I'm going on a field trip with my _____ class. We're studying landforms.

5. A student must maintain a _____ level of acceptable work to be successful.

Practice

A. Learn the words.

Key Vocabulary

melt	to change from a solid to a liquid state
upward	toward a higher level
edge	the line along which two surfaces meet
eruption	the ejection of magma and gases onto the Earth's surface

TOEFL Vocabulary

continent	a large landmass such, as Africa or North America
consequence	a result
apart	separated; away from each other
range	a series
considerable	significant or large in amount or degree

Reading Passage

B. Read the passage and underline the key information.

Earth's Plate

The continents of the Earth seem to fit together like a big puzzle. That is because the Earth's outer layer, called the crust, is divided into smaller sections, called plates. These plates move around very slowly, but their movement has big consequences.

When the plates move apart, the space that is left behind is filled with hot magma that comes up from the inside of the Earth. Magma is very hot rock. It is so hot that it has melted and become a liquid. It then cools and forms a new crust.

This does not mean that the Earth is getting any bigger. ■ 1) When two plates move apart, they crash into other plates on the other side. This is how large mountain ranges are formed. The plates have nowhere to go, so they push upward against each other and form mountains.

Sometimes, one plate's edge sinks below the other plate's edge. ■ 2) This creates a deep hole. If the plate sinks a considerable distance, it could result in hot magma eruptions. This is how volcanoes are formed. ■ 3) Finally, the movements of these plates can be the cause of earthquakes. This is why most earthquakes occur at the edges of these moving plates. ■ 4)

C. Choose the correct answers.

1. **Directions:** An introductory sentence for a brief summary of the passage is provided below. Complete the summary by selecting the THREE answer choices that express the most important ideas in the passage. Some sentences do not belong in the summary because they express ideas that are not presented in the passage or are minor ideas in the passage.

   The shape of the Earth is constantly changing because the plates are drifting.

   Answer Choices

   (A) Hot magma is the cause of volcanic eruptions.
   (B) The Earth is divided into plates that drift apart and collide with one another.
   (C) Plates that are drifting apart cause earthquakes.
   (D) Plates that collide result in mountain ranges and volcanoes.
   (E) When plates drift apart, new crust is created.

2. Look at the four squares [■] that indicate where the following sentence could be added to the passage.

   As magma is erupted, it then cools and becomes solid, and the volcano gets bigger each time there is a new eruption.

   Where would the sentence best fit?

   (A) Square 1   (B) Square 2
   (C) Square 3   (D) Square 4

TOEFL Vocabulary Practice

D. Fill in the blanks with the correct words.

continent	apart	range	consequence	considerable

1. She has been training for months and now she can run a _____ distance.

2. I have visited every _____ except Antarctica.

3. You can see that this mountain _____ is very old because the hills are small and round.

4. You should let an expert take your computer _____ to fix it.

5. One _____ of eating too much is that you will become overweight.

Read the passage.

The Grand Canyon

The Grand Canyon is a great place for people who are interested in geology. The Colorado River has been flowing through the canyon for a very long time. Because of this, it has caused considerable erosion. One positive aspect of this erosion is that it has created beautiful and fascinating landforms. We can identify the rock and learn about the history of the Earth in that region.

We have learned many things from the Grand Canyon. ■ **1)** Millions of years ago, the Earth looked much different. ■ **2)** Much of the western part of the North American continent was under water. What is now the Grand Canyon was flat land. ■ **3)** The Colorado River ran through this land. However, two plates crashed and they created a mountain range. ■ **4)** We now call this mountain range the Rocky Mountains. The new hills meant that the river flowed with more force. For the next six million years, it flowed through the rocks. This is what created the Grand Canyon. However, wind, rain, and ice also helped. Together, they shaped one of the most impressive natural physical features on Earth.

The erosion of the rock has exposed layers of different types of rock. Each section of rock has its own consistent composition. That's how we can tell the layers apart. We know that there was once a large mountain range there. Over time, it was worn down. Eventually, the land became flat again. Then, the sea came in. This caused a new layer of rock to form. The sea brought in deposits of minerals. When the sea level dropped, the minerals stayed behind. Therefore, a new layer of rock was formed. Then, the Rocky Mountains were formed because of the movement of the plates. As a consequence, the Grand Canyon was created. It is a very beautiful sight.

Choose the correct answers.

1. The word it in paragraph 1 refers to

   (A) the Grand Canyon   (B) geology

   (C) the Colorado River   (D) erosion

2. Which of the following best expresses the essential information in the highlighted sentence? Incorrect answers change the meaning in important ways or leave out essential information.

   We can identify the rock and learn about the history of the Earth in that region.

   (A) By determining rock type, we can learn about the past.
   (B) By studying history, we can determine rock types.
   (C) The past gives us clues to the future of the region.
   (D) We can make guesses about the history of the region.

3. Look at the four squares [■] that indicate where the following sentence could be added to the passage.

The continents were shaped differently and found at different locations.

Where would the sentence best fit?

(A) Square 1   (B) Square 2

(C) Square 3   (D) Square 4

4. According to the passage, which of the following was NOT a cause of the landforms at the Grand Canyon?

(A) River   (B) Wind

(C) Ice   (D) Earthquakes

5. Which of the following can be inferred about the Colorado River?

(A) It helped create the Rocky Mountains.

(B) It is an important source of water in the dry region.

(C) It was the dominant force shaping the Grand Canyon.

(D) It would not have been created if there was no Grand Canyon.

6. Directions: An introductory sentence for a brief summary of the passage is provided below. Complete the summary by selecting the THREE answer choices that express the most important ideas in the passage. Some sentences do not belong in the summary because they express ideas that are not presented in the passage or are minor ideas in the passage.

The Grand Canyon is both beautiful and fascinating.

Answer Choices

(A) Its landforms have been carved mainly by the Colorado River.

(B) The Colorado River was not always as wide as it is today.

(C) Erosion has exposed layers of rock from which we can learn much.

(D) The second layer of rock was formed as the North American plate drifted south.

(E) Layers of rock were created by shifting continents and changing sea levels.

Check-up

A. Choose the correct answers.

1. When you come to a summary question, you should
   (A) leave sections of the chart blank if you're not sure of the correct answers
   (B) select the three answer choices that represent the most important points of the passage
   (C) choose the three answer choices that include minor details from the passage
   (D) choose the three answer choices that contradict details from the passage

Key Vocabulary Practice

B. Fill in the blanks with the correct words.

minerals	composition	texture	landforms
eruption	melts	edge	upward

1. You have to put the ice cream in the freezer before it _____.

2. The 1980 _____ of Mount St. Helens in the United States killed 57 people.

3. Gold is one of the most valuable _____.

4. NASA scientists were eager to study the _____ of the rocks brought back from the moon.

5. Silk is a soft material with a very smooth _____.

6. The aircraft had to climb _____ to avoid hitting the mountain.

7. Badlands National Park in South Dakota consists of such _____ as sharply eroded buttes, pinnacles, and spires blended with the largest protected mixed grass prairie in the United States.

8. The student's pencil rolled off the _____ of the table.

[Review 1]

Read the passage.

Orchids

If you are a botany student, you may learn about a special group of plants. It is the biggest group of plants that can have flowers. This special plant group is called orchids. There are approximately 22,000 different kinds of orchids. That is a considerable amount. Every year scientists identify about 800 new kinds. The scientists go into forests. They go up mountains. They spend months looking around for new plants. These investigations help them find new orchids.

There is a very large range of these plants on Earth. They are distributed all over the world. They grow on most continents. ■ 1) They grow in Asia, North America, South America, Africa, Europe, and Australia. ■ 2) Most grow in the hottest regions of the world. ■ 3) We call these hot places the tropics. ■ 4) The dense rainforests of South America and Asia are in the tropics. Orchids do not grow in deserts. They need a lot of water to grow well.

Orchids usually have very bright flowers. These flowers have a very distinct look. They are very beautiful and interesting to look at. You can find orchids in almost every color. Some are large and some are small. They also have a distinct smell or scent. The scent is used to make perfume. The flowers are seasonal. They bloom in the spring and summer.

Orchids are a very ancient plant species. They have been around for millions of years. They have grown on the Earth since the time of the dinosaurs.

Choose the correct answers.

1. The word botany in paragraph 1 is closest in meaning to

(A) general science   (B) plant history

(C) plant science   (D) geography

2. According to the passage, scientists find new orchids by

(A) working in laboratories

(B) searching in people's gardens

(C) spending time in Asia and Africa

(D) traveling through jungles and mountain ranges

3. Which of the following best expresses the essential information in the highlighted sentence? Incorrect answers change the meaning in important ways or leave out essential information.

There is a very large range of these plants on Earth.

(A) There is a big variety of different kinds of orchids available.
(B) Earth is not the only place orchids grow but has the most kinds.
(C) The largest range of orchids grows in soil, not rock.
(D) Orchids are giant plants that have big roots systems.

4. Look at the four squares [■] that indicate where the following sentence could be added to the passage.

They do not grow on Antarctica.

Where would the sentence best fit?

(A) Square 1   (B) Square 2
(C) Square 3   (D) Square 4

5. According to paragraph 3, which of the following can be inferred about orchid flowers?

(A) All orchid flowers look the same.
(B) Orchids don't flower in fall and winter.
(C) They are always very expensive.
(D) All perfume contains orchid scent.

6. According to the passage, all of the following is true of orchids EXCEPT

(A) they grow on all seven continents
(B) most orchids grow in tropical regions
(C) they have grown on Earth for millennia
(D) they are used in the perfume industry

Read the passage.

The Egyptian Pyramids

Pyramids are very big stone structures. They are shaped like triangles. They were built between 4000 and 5000 years ago in Egypt. The first pyramids were built in a period called the Old Kingdom. At this time, Egypt was a great civilization. The last pyramids were built in a period called the Middle Kingdom.

Egypt was a great desert empire. It had very rich and powerful rulers. These rulers were kings with a special name. They were called pharaohs. When they died, they were buried in the pyramids. Pyramids are royal tombs.

The Egyptians were very religious. They believed in life after death. They thought the kings would wake up in the pyramids after they had been buried. They believed the kings would keep on living inside the pyramids. They thought the kings would need clothes and jewels for this second life. They buried the kings with many wonderful things. They also buried the kings with many slaves. The slaves were locked inside the pyramids. The slaves were still alive. Egyptians thought they would serve the kings when they woke up. This was a tradition.

Many scientists have explored inside the pyramids. ■ 1) There are many tunnels inside them. ■ 2) They are made of sandstone blocks. ■ 3) No one is really sure how Egyptians built the pyramids. ■ 4) Their construction is a mystery. No one knows who the architects were who thought up the idea. No one knows if slaves built them, or knows if skilled workers built them. No one knows what building techniques were used. All they know is that it took hard physical labor. For now, scientists can only guess how it was done.

Choose the correct answers.

1. The word structures in paragraph 1 is closest in meaning to

(A) triangles　　　　　　　　　(B) temples

(C) buildings　　　　　　　　　(D) tombs

2. Which of the following best expresses the essential information in the highlighted sentence? Incorrect answers change the meaning in important ways or leave out essential information.

At this time, Egypt was a great civilization.

(A) Egyptians were learning civil engineering at this time.
(B) Egypt was very advanced kingdom in these years.
(C) Over time, Egypt had become a very big country.
(D) Egypt was a great destination for travelers during this period.

3. The word they in paragraph 3 refers to

(A) Egyptian pharaohs   (B) Egyptian scientists
(C) Egyptian people   (D) Egyptian slaves

4. Why does the author mention that slaves were buried alive inside the pyramids?

(A) To show how cruel and evil Egyptians were
(B) To show how much power the pharaohs had
(C) To explain what traditions the Egyptians had when they buried a pharaoh
(D) To infer how little slaves' lives were valued

5. Look at the four squares [■] that indicate where the following sentence could be added to the passage.

Each one is very large and extremely heavy.

Where would the sentence best fit?

(A) Square 1   (B) Square 2
(C) Square 3   (D) Square 4

6. According to paragraph 4, which of the following is true?

(A) Scientists cannot be sure how the Egyptians built the pyramids.
(B) Scientists think one architect designed all the pyramids.
(C) Many scientists have died inside the pyramids.
(D) Scientists know skilled laborers built the pyramids.

Read the passage.

Gold

Gold is a precious metal. It is precious because it is not easy to find. It is a metal because it is very hard. It also melts at a high temperature.

Gold is an element. There are 117 different elements. Some are metals. Some are gases. Some are rocks. An element is something that is pure. It is not mixed with something else. It occurs in nature in its simplest form. Elements are made of atoms. Scientists specify whether something is an element or a compound. A compound is something made of many different elements. The elements are mixed together. Scientists do tests to establish if something is an element. There are more compounds than elements.

Since ancient times, man has consistently used gold to trade with. We have also used it to make jewelry and coins. Long ago, gold coins were used as money. Today, we use paper money and our coins are made from cheap metals. Gold is not cheap. Many people like to buy loved ones gold jewelry as gifts. Such items are a big expense.

Gold is found inside rocks deep under the ground. Scientists have to look hard to find it. First, they have to study rocks at university. They also have to learn about how gold is formed. The study of rocks and metals is called geology.

These scientists are often employed by gold mines to find new gold deposits. Mining companies finance their searches. The mines have big budgets for these searches. That is because gold is so valuable. If scientists find new gold deposits, the mine owners can become very rich. That is why they spend a lot of money looking for gold. They don't always find it!

Choose the correct answers.

1. According to the passage, which of the following is true of gold?

   (A) It is an element and a kind of rock.
   (B) It is an element and a precious metal.
   (C) It is a compound and a kind of rock.
   (D) It is a compound and a precious metal.

2. What can be inferred from paragraph 3 about the coins we use today?

   (A) They are made from cheap gold.
   (B) They are not made of gold.
   (C) They are worth a lot of money.
   (D) They are very old.

3. The pronoun their in paragraph 5 refers to

(A) gold mines
(B) scientists
(C) gold miners
(D) jewelers

4. All of the following are true of gold mine owners EXCEPT

(A) they pay scientists to look for gold
(B) they spend a lot of money looking for gold
(C) they consistently locate gold
(D) they can become very rich if they find gold deposits

5. Why does the author tell us that scientists don't always find gold?

(A) Because she thinks it is funny
(B) Because she wants to show that science is not always accurate
(C) To emphasize how rare gold is
(D) Because she is glad gold mines cannot always get rich from mining

6. Complete the table below by selecting the appropriate phrases from the answer choices and match them to the category they fit best. TWO of the answer choices will NOT be used. The question is worth 3 points.

Answer choices

(A) Made of atoms
(B) Makes jewelry
(C) Precious compound
(D) Kind of metal
(E) One of 117 elements
(F) Trade and coinage
(G) To make paper money

Chemical properties of gold

- _____
- _____
- _____

Uses of gold

- _____
- _____

[07] Literature

Getting Ready to Read

A. Learn the words.

Key Vocabulary

poet	a writer of verse
district	a territory; an area of land
poem	a piece of writing written in verse
prelude	an event or action that introduces or occurs before something more important

TOEFL Vocabulary

celebrate	to honor and praise, often with a party
shift	a change in thinking or feeling; a move
approach	a way of doing something; to move toward
philosophy	a way of thinking; a belief system
state	to speak; to say

B. Learn the question types.

TOEFL Question Types

Vocabulary

The word X in the passage is closest in meaning to...
In stating X, the author means that...

- This question asks for the meaning of a word in the context of how it is used in the passage.
- The word is usually important for understanding part of the passage.
- When you choose your answer, ensure that the sentence still makes sense with that answer substituted in.

Reference

The word X in the passage refers to...

- The referent (word being referred to) is not always the noun closest to the pronoun being asked about.
- The referent usually comes before the word being asked about.
- When you choose your answer, ensure that the sentence still makes sense with that answer substituted in.

C. Read the passage. Number each paragraph with the correct main idea or purpose.

> 1. Information on Wordsworth's most famous work
> 2. Information on Wordsworth's philosophy
> 3. Information on Wordsworth's early life
> 4. Information on Wordsworth's poetry topics

William Wordsworth

___William Wordsworth was a famous English poet. He was born in 1770 and died in 1850. He grew up in a very beautiful part of England. It is called the Lake District.

___Wordsworth loved nature. He wanted to celebrate England's natural beauty. He wrote hundreds of poems about flowers, birds, lakes, and old buildings.

___His poems caused a shift in English literature. He took a new approach to writing. This was in reaction to the philosophy that stated feelings were not important. Wordsworth believed that emotions and feelings were more important than thoughts. His writings showed this belief.

___Perhaps his most famous poem is called *The Prelude*. It was not published until after his death. It is a very long poem about his life. It tells the reader how and why he became a poet. The poem starts when Wordsworth is a boy. It ends when he is an adult.

Note-taking

D. Complete the summary notes by filling in the blanks.

Topic:	William Wordsworth
Introduction:	Famous English _____.
	Born 1770 and died _____.
	Grew up in beautiful _____.
Poems:	Wanted to _____ England's beauty.
	Wrote about flowers, _____, lakes, and old _____.
Philosophy:	His poems caused a _____.
	Reacted against idea that _____ not important.
	Believed _____ and feelings most important.
Famous work:	Poem called _____.
	_____ after his death.
	Poem tells why Wordsworth became a _____.
	Starts—He's a _____.
	Finishes—He's an _____.

E. Choose the correct answers.

1. The word shift in the passage is closest in meaning to

(A) a change   (B) a fight

2. The word philosophy in the passage is closest in meaning to

(A) a belief   (B) a law

3. The pronoun this in paragraph 3 refers to

(A) his love of nature   (B) his new approach

4. The pronoun it paragraph 4 refers to

(A) the poem   (B) the poet

TOEFL Vocabulary Practice

F. Fill in the blanks with the correct words.

shift	philosophy	stated	celebrated	approach

1. After World War II, there was a big _____ in world politics.

2. Albert Einstein had a different _____ to studying mathematics.

3. Confucianism is a famous Asian _____.

4. Christmas is _____ in many different countries.

5. The teacher _____ that the homework would be due next week.

Practice

A. Learn the words.

Key Vocabulary

novel	a book that tells a story
rude	ill-mannered; not polite
explain	to give reason for something
liar	a person who is not truthful

TOEFL Vocabulary

pride	an opinion of yourself that you are better than others
prejudice	an opinion without knowing
realize	to understand
assume	to think something without knowing
demonstrate	to show

Reading Passage

B. Read the passage and underline the key information.

Pride and Prejudice

Pride and Prejudice is a very famous novel. It was written by Jane Austen and it was published in 1813. The novel is humorous. It is also a love story.

The story is about a proud man called Darcy. He falls in love with a girl called Elizabeth. At first, Darcy is very rude to Elizabeth. Therefore, she doesn't like him. Then a man called Wickham tells Elizabeth that Darcy is not a good man. He tells Elizabeth many lies about Darcy. She assumes that Wickham is telling the truth.

Darcy starts to communicate with Elizabeth. He writes her many letters. The letters explain why he seems rude. He is a very shy man. He often says rude things. However, he does not mean them.

Darcy also tells Elizabeth that Wickham is a liar. Then Wickham runs away with Elizabeth's younger sister. Now Elizabeth realizes that Darcy was telling the truth.

As we read more of the novel, we discover that Darcy is actually very kind. He does many things to demonstrate this. He helps Elizabeth's family. He saves her sister.

The story has a happy conclusion. Elizabeth falls in love with Darcy. They get married.

C. Choose the correct answers.

1. The word rude in paragraph 2 is closest in meaning to

(A) kind   (B) unkind

2. The pronoun he in paragraph 3 refers to

(A) Wickham   (B) Darcy

3. An introductory sentence for a brief summary of the passage is provided below. Complete the summary by selecting the THREE answer choices that express the most important ideas in the passage. Some sentences do not belong in the summary because they express ideas that are not presented in the passage or are minor ideas in the passage.

Pride and Prejudice is a funny novel that teaches us you can't judge a book by its cover.

Answer Choices

(A) Elizabeth falls in love with Wickham because he saved her from Darcy.
(B) Elizabeth has poor opinion of Darcy because of how he acts when they first meet.
(C) Elizabeth begins to realize that Darcy is a very kind man.
(D) Darcy tells Elizabeth lies about Wickham because he is jealous.
(E) Elizabeth falls in love with Darcy when she realizes his true nature.

D. Fill in the blanks with the correct words.

realize	assumed	pride	prejudice	demonstrated

1. Napoleon wrongly _____ that his army was stronger than Nelson's.

2. Students should _____ the importance of doing their homework.

3. Too much _____ can be a negative character trait.

4. Escape artist Harry Houdini often _____ his ability with daring escapes.

5. In some places in the world, _____ based on race is still a problem.

Read the passage.

Science Fiction

There were many changes in the world in the nineteenth century. There was a big shift in scientific philosophy. Scientists began to create new machines. This excited many writers and made an impression on them. Writers wished to celebrate these scientific changes. They started writing stories about science. This literature became known as science fiction.

Science fiction stories took a new approach. Writers didn't write about the past or the present. Instead, they wrote about the future. They wrote make-believe novels. They wrote about the power of science. They wanted to demonstrate that science made great things possible.

These writers believed that man would someday build spaceships and travel in space. They also assumed that people would visit far away planets. They often wrote that space travelers met strange life forms or aliens. The humans would communicate with the aliens. They would learn about their worlds. They would learn about their cultures. In these stories, they sometimes stated that the aliens were unfriendly.

One of the best known early science fiction writers was H.G. Wells. Wells was an English writer, who lived in England. ■ **1)** The scientists in England were very smart. ■ **2)** They made many new machines. ■ **3)** His most famous novel is called *The War of the Worlds*. It was published in 1898. ■ **4)**

The novel is about aliens who attack the Earth. The aliens are from Mars. They kill many people but then they get sick. In the end, the aliens die. The aliens realize that they cannot live on Earth because the air makes them sick. It is explained that the common cold is very deadly to the aliens.

Wells also wrote a story about time travel. This novel is called *The Time Machine*. It is about a man who builds a time machine and travels to the future.

Choose the correct answers.

1. The word scientists in paragraph 1 is closest in meaning to
   (A) builders
   (B) inventors
   (C) writers
   (D) aliens

2. According to the passage, which is NOT true about science fiction stories?
   (A) They were about the future.
   (B) They were about the present.
   (C) They were about the power of science.
   (D) They were make-believe.

3. Which of the following best expresses the essential information in the highlighted sentence? Incorrect answers change the meaning in important ways or leave out essential information.

They wanted to demonstrate that science made great things possible.

(A) The writers wished to show people the wonder of science.
(B) They wanted to warn people about the danger of science.
(C) The writers wanted to illustrate that science was difficult.
(D) They dreamed of doing wonderful things through science.

4. Which of the following can be inferred about the writer, H.G. Wells?

(A) He wanted to be a scientist.
(B) He was scared of scientists.
(C) He thought science was very exciting.
(D) He wanted to be a space traveler.

5. Look at the four squares [■] that indicate where the following sentence could be added to the passage.

Their work gave Wells many good ideas for his novels.

Where would the sentence best fit?

(A) Square 1   (B) Square 2
(C) Square 3   (D) Square 4

6. Directions: An introductory sentence for a brief summary of the passage is provided below. Complete the summary by selecting the THREE answer choices that express the most important ideas in the passage. Some sentences do not belong in the summary because they express ideas that are not presented in the passage or are minor ideas in the passage.

With the scientific advances of the late nineteenth century, a new literature, called science fiction, was born.

Answer choices

(A) These books were titled *The War of the Worlds* and *The Time Machine*.
(B) Writers imagined that space travelers would meet and communicate with aliens.
(C) There were many great scientists in England at this time.
(D) Writers took a new approach, writing about the future, space, and time travel.
(E) An English writer called H.G. Wells wrote two famous novels on these subjects.

Check-up

A. Choose the correct answers.

1. When you come to a vocabulary question, you should
   (A) select the answer that has the same sounds as the highlighted word
   (B) choose the antonym of the highlighted word
   (C) select the answer that contradicts the highlighted word
   (D) choose the synonym of the highlighted word

2. What should you do when answering a reference question?
   (A) Eliminate all choices that occur before the pronoun in question.
   (B) Select the word that is a synonym to the pronoun in question.
   (C) Ensure the sentence still makes sense with your answer in place of the pronoun being asked about.
   (D) Choose the word closest to the pronoun being asked about.

Key Vocabulary Practice

B. Fill in the blanks with the correct words.

novel	rude	district	prelude
explain	poet	liar	poem

1. Talking on your cell phone in the movie theater is _____ behavior.

2. The directions that come with the machine _____ how to use it.

3. Robert Frost is a famous American _____.

4. The "DC" in Washington DC stands for _____ of Columbia.

5. An undersea earthquake is often the _____ to a tidal wave.

6. A person who doesn't tell the truth is a _____.

7. *In Flanders Field* is a famous _____ about World War I.

8. *Moby Dick* is often called the great American _____.

[08] Environment

Getting Ready to Read

A. Learn the words.

Key Vocabulary

rainforest	a forest or jungle found in a tropical region
filter	something that removes particles from the substance passing through it
as such	what is indicated; applicable to the situation
harm	to damage or injure

TOEFL Vocabulary

species	a specific type of living thing
habitat	the area in which a plant or animal lives
extinct	no longer in existence
program	a planned set of actions
poverty	the condition of being poor

B. Learn the question types.

TOEFL Question Types

Factual Information
According to the paragraph, which of the following is true of X?
The author's description of X mentions which of the following?
According to the information in paragraph 1, why did X do Y?

- Eliminate answer choices you immediately recognize as incorrect.
- Scan the paragraph or section mentioned in the question for the relevant details.
- Incorrect answer choices may contain other details from the passage, so ensure the answer you choose contains the correct details to answer that specific question.

Negative Factual Information
According to the passage, which of the following is NOT true of X?
The author's description of X mentions all of the following EXCEPT...

- Scan the entire passage for the details mentioned in the answer choices.
- The correct answer choice is either not mentioned in the passage at all, or it contradicts a correct statement or detail that is mentioned.

C. Read the passage. Number each paragraph with the correct main idea or purpose.

> 1. Information on how damage to the rainforests affects wildlife and their habitat
> 2. Information on the impact of deforestation
> 3. Suggestions for saving the rainforests
> 4. Information on some of the causes of deforestation
> 5. Information on the importance of the rainforests to our climate

Deforestation

___The rainforests are needed to keep the air clean. Trees act as filters. They clean pollution from the air. When we cut down trees, we lose these filters. This affects our climate.

___Many species of plants and animals live in the rainforest. Deforestation results in damage to their habitat. While they are not extinct as such, many animals are in danger of becoming so.

___Deforestation occurs for several reasons. Large companies make money by using the resources of the rainforests. Poor farmers must cut down trees to make farmland.

___The impact of deforestation is serious. When forests are cut down, the air quality is harmed. Animals lose their homes. We also lose a great deal of potential knowledge.

___We can save the rainforests through our choices. We can choose not to support companies who harm them. Programs to end poverty in poor countries can also help.

Note-taking

D. Complete the summary notes by filling in the blanks.

Topic:	Deforestation
Introduction:	_____ keep the air clean.
	Trees _____ pollution from the air.
	The loss of trees affects the _____.
Negative effects:	Deforestation damages _____.
	Many animals may become _____.
Causes:	Deforestation is caused by large _____ and poor _____.
Result:	_____ results in poor air quality and loss of _____ knowledge.
Solutions:	Don't support companies that _____ the rainforest.
	Programs to end _____.

E. Choose the correct answers.

1. According to the passage, climate change occurs because
(A) trees act as filters to clean the air
(B) deforestation deprives the air of natural filters

2. According to the passage, why are rainforest animals becoming extinct?
(A) Because logging activity disrupts mating
(B) Because their homes are being destroyed

3. According to the passage, which of the following is NOT mentioned as a cause of deforestation?
(A) The rising popularity of medicinal herbs
(B) The poverty that exists in some forested areas

4. According to the passage, which of the following is NOT mentioned as a drawback of deforestation?
(A) An economic recession causing a rise in poverty rates
(B) A loss of natural habitat causing extinction for animals

TOEFL Vocabulary Practice

F. Fill in the blanks with the correct words.

| poverty | extinct | species | program | habitat |

1. The U.N. is doing what it can to ease _____ in the third world.

2. The dodo bird became _____ in 1681.

3. The new recycling _____ has been very successful.

4. Wetlands are the natural _____ of many different types of birds.

5. The team discovered a new _____ of frog.

Practice

A. Learn the words.

Key Vocabulary

cut back	to reduce something
limit	to set a standard that cannot be exceeded
threat	a danger to safety or security
endanger	to put in danger

TOEFL Vocabulary

consume	to use up
campaign	a set of activities aimed at reaching a goal
fund	to provide money for something
rely	to depend on
conserve	to save for future use; to use wisely

Reading Passage

B. Read the passage and underline the key information.

Water Conservation

We should not consume more water than we actually need. If we do, we won't have enough water in the future. However, just how much is too much? If we remove more fresh water than nature replaces, we have taken too much.

Many cities run campaigns to get people to stop wasting water. They show them ways they can cut back on water use. They also increase water bills for people who use too much. In addition, they fund programs that reduce water use. For example, they give people shower heads and toilets that use less water. Finally, they make laws limiting the amount of water people can use.

Another threat to our water supply is pollution. When our sources of fresh water get polluted, we can no longer use this water. This also endangers the animals that rely on the water.

There are several things we can all do to conserve water. We can save lots of water by not letting the tap run while we brush our teeth. By keeping a bottle of water in the refrigerator, we can save water. This is because the water stays cold. We don't have to let the water run until it gets cold.

C. Choose the correct answers.

1. Which of the following is a major threat to our water supply?

(A) Pollution   (B) Governments

2. Which of the following was NOT mentioned as a way governments encourage people to use less water?

(A) Increasing the price   (B) Cutting off water supply

3. The word fresh in the passage is closest in meaning to

(A) ripe   (B) not salty

4. The word them in paragraph 2 refers to

(A) cities   (B) people

TOEFL Vocabulary Practice

D. Fill in the blanks with the correct words.

consume	campaign	fund	conserve	rely

1. Some students receive scholarships in order to _____ their education.

2. The governor is planning an aggressive _____ for reelection.

3. Plants _____ on the Sun for energy.

4. I'm looking for a smaller car that doesn't _____ so much gas.

5. It is important that we _____ water for the future.

Test

Read the passage.

Hybrid Cars

Many people rely on cars to get around. This can be a problem for two reasons. The first is that cars cause pollution. With so many cars on the road, the quality of the air that we breathe is reduced. The Earth is our habitat and we must protect it. The second is that cars run on fuel, which comes from oil. There is a limited amount of oil in the world. When our oil runs out, we cannot replace it. Therefore, we should try to conserve oil.

■ 1) One solution is to design cars that consume less fuel. The most efficient cars today are called hybrids. They run on gas and electricity. They save energy by turning off the engine when the car is not moving. ■ 2) They don't waste gas when they are stuck in traffic. The electricity source is a battery. ■ 3) It recharges itself when the driver uses the brake. That way, the driver never has to plug the car in to charge it. Hybrids also have smaller engines. ■ 4) This means they use less gas. They can go twenty-five to forty percent further on the same amount of gas as a normal car.

Pollution results in global warming, which causes climate change. This can endanger life on Earth. One example of this is the many species of animals that are becoming extinct. As such, there is a global campaign aimed at limiting the amount of pollution we produce. Switching to hybrid cars is a major goal. Sadly, not everyone cares about clean air. They do, however, care about money. As gas prices rise, hybrid cars look more attractive. Some governments fund programs to make hybrids even more attractive. They offer tax cuts to people who buy them. One day, hybrid cars could replace normal cars as the standard vehicle around the world.

Choose the correct answers.

1. According to the passage, which of the following is NOT mentioned as a way that hybrids save fuel?

   (A) They don't waste gas when they're not moving.
   (B) They run on bio-fuel.
   (C) They have small engines.
   (D) They generate their own electricity.

2. Look at the four squares [■] that indicate where the following sentence could be added to the passage.

   Most car engines today are far bigger than they need to be.

   Where would the sentence best fit?

   (A) Square 1   (B) Square 2
   (C) Square 3   (D) Square 4

3. Which of the following best expresses the essential information in the highlighted sentence? Incorrect answers change the meaning in important ways or leave out essential information.

They can go twenty-five to forty percent further on the same amount of gas as a normal car.

(A) They use less electricity than regular cars.
(B) They are faster than regular cars.
(C) They last longer than regular cars.
(D) They can travel further than regular cars on the same amount of gas.

4. The word this in paragraph 3 refers to
(A) cars
(B) gasoline
(C) climate change
(D) the Earth

5. Why does the author mention financial incentives for buying a hybrid?
(A) To demonstrate that hybrids are a wise option for anyone
(B) To suggest that hybrids should be made more affordable
(C) To imply that poor people are not concerned about the environment
(D) To show that only environmentalists are willing to buy hybrids

6. Directions: An introductory sentence for a brief summary of the passage is provided below. Complete the summary by selecting the THREE answer choices that express the most important ideas in the passage. Some sentences do not belong in the summary because they express ideas that are not presented in the passage or are minor ideas in the passage.

One way to reduce the danger of pollution is to promote the use of hybrid vehicles.

Answer choices
(A) Hybrid cars burn less fuel, so they create less pollution.
(B) Hybrid cars are cheaper to run.
(C) Hybrid cars use both gas and electricity.
(D) Hybrid cars are three times as fast as regular cars.
(E) Governments offer tax cuts to hybrid vehicle owners.

Check-up

A. Choose the correct answers.

1. What should you do when you come to a factual information question?
   (A) Reread the entire passage for all of the relevant information.
   (B) Select the choice that can best be inferred from information in the passage.
   (C) Choose all answers that are mentioned in the passage.
   (D) Select the factual information explicitly mentioned in the passage.

2. For negative factual information questions, you should
   (A) select an answer choice that contradicts a detail mentioned in the passage
   (B) scan the passage for similar information to that in question
   (C) look through the passage for the same information but worded differently
   (D) choose an answer choice that supports the main idea of the passage

Key Vocabulary Practice

B. Fill in the blanks with the correct words.

rainforests	filter	harm	as such
limiting	threat	cut back	endanger

1. You have to clean the water _____ in your aquarium or your fish will die.

2. You must cover up on sunny days because UV rays can _____ your skin.

3. The whale shark is not a "whale" _____; it is actually a fish.

4. One of the most _____ factors to putting a vehicle in space is weight.

5. The _____ of global warming has many people considering alternative energy sources.

6. In order to lose weight, you should _____ on the number of calories you consume each day.

7. The _____ of the Amazon River basin contain thousands of species of plants and animals.

8. Airport workers try to keep birds away from the runways because they can _____ planes trying to land or take off.

[09] Health

Getting Ready to Read

A. Learn the words.

Key Vocabulary

awake	not asleep
well-being	a state of overall health and happiness
disturbed	upset; interfered with
immune system	the bodily processes that protect the body from illness and help it recover

TOEFL Vocabulary

adequate	enough; sufficient
constitute	to establish; to make up
vary	to change
concentrate	to focus
coordination	the act of different elements working together smoothly; the ability of body parts to work together well

B. Learn the question type.

TOEFL Question Type

Sentence Simplification
Which of the following best expresses the essential information in the highlighted sentence? *Incorrect* answers change the meaning in important ways or leave out essential information.

- Look for synonyms of words in the highlighted passage in the answer choices.
- Ensure that the most important details of the highlighted passage are in the answer choice you choose, even if the sentence structure is different.
- Be careful to choose the answer choice that both contains the same important details and makes the same point as the highlighted passage.

C. Read the passage. Number each paragraph with the correct main idea or purpose.

> 1. How much sleep we need
> 2. What the passage is about
> 3. The impact of sleep on mental health
> 4. The impact of sleep on physical health

The Importance of Sleep

___We spend about one third of our lives asleep because we need it to work properly. When we don't get adequate sleep at night, we have problems when we are awake.

___How many hours constitute a good night's sleep? This can vary from person to person. But on average, most people need at least eight hours per night. Some need more, and some need less.

___Sleep affects our health and well-being. When we are tired, we find it difficult to concentrate. We may become overly emotional and experience some stress. Unfortunately, this stress can make it difficult to get more sleep.

___Our physical well-being is also disturbed by lack of sleep. When we don't get enough sleep, we may get headaches and our coordination suffers. When we have enough sleep, we are faster and stronger. Our immune systems also work better. That means that we are less likely to get sick.

D. Complete the summary notes by filling in the blanks.

Topic:	The Importance of Sleep
Introduction:	One _____ of our lives spent sleeping.
	Need it to _____ properly.
	Less than _____ = problems when _____.
Amount needed:	Amount of sleep needed varies.
	Average is _____ hours.
Reasons needed:	Sleep affects _____ and well-being.
	Tired people can't _____ and may become
	_____.
	This makes it _____ to sleep.
Effects:	Lack of sleep results in _____ and _____ problems.
	Sleep makes us _____.
	Helps our _____ keep us from getting sick.

E. Choose the correct answers.

1. Which of the following best expresses the essential information in the highlighted sentence? Incorrect answers change the meaning in important ways or leave out essential information.

We spend about one third of our lives asleep because we need it to work properly.

(A) We must sleep half the time so we won't make mistakes.
(B) We must sleep for one third of the time in order to perform well.

2. Which of the following best expresses the essential information in the highlighted sentence? Incorrect answers change the meaning in important ways or leave out essential information.

When we don't get enough sleep, we may get headaches and our coordination suffers.

(A) Inadequate sleep causes headaches and clumsiness.
(B) Oversleeping makes your head hurt.

TOEFL Vocabulary Practice

F. Fill in the blanks with the correct words.

adequate	concentrate	constitutes	vary	coordination

1. You should study in a quiet place so that you can _____.

2. Drinking and driving is illegal because alcohol impairs judgment and

_____.

3. An effective exercise program should _____ the activities you do every day.

4. A bowl of granola with fruit and yogurt _____ a healthy breakfast.

5. You should make sure you have _____ lighting when studying so you don't strain your eyes.

Practice

A. Learn the words.

Key Vocabulary

fast food	processed food prepared quickly
calorie	a unit of measurement of the energy derived from food
popularity	admiration or approval of someone or something by people in general
overweight	heavier than the ideal weight

TOEFL Vocabulary

negative	bad; unfavorable
feature	to have or include as an important characteristic
involve	to include or contain
attitude	the way a person feels about a certain thing
insist	to demand

Reading Passage

B. Read the passage and underline the key information.

Fast Food

The fast food business has had a negative effect on America. Food that is quick and convenient is bad for you. People like it, though, because it tastes good. It is also very cheap. Finally, it is great for people with busy lives. When you don't have time to cook, fast food seems like a good choice.

Most fast food meals feature a hamburger, French fries, and a soda. There may be some lettuce or a tomato on the burger. But this is less than a full serving of vegetables. The meal is high in calories. It is also high in fat. Since it is low in vitamins, it makes you feel tired. That means that you are not likely to burn off the extra fat.

Fast food companies spend a lot of money on ads. These ads involve themes that children like. Children then have the attitude that fast food is fun. They grow up thinking that fast food is good.

The popularity of fast food has changed America. Many people, including children, are overweight. People should stop buying fast food. We can also insist that fast food restaurants offer a wider selection of healthy choices.

C. Choose the correct answers.

1. Which of the following best expresses the essential information in the highlighted sentence? Incorrect answers change the meaning in important ways or leave out essential information.

When you don't have time to cook, fast food seems like a good choice.

(A) Fast food is the best option available for busy people.
(B) Fast food appeals to busy people.

2. According to the author, why does fast food leave you feeling tired?

(A) It is low in vitamins.   (B) It is high in vitamins.

3. According to the passage, which of the following is NOT mentioned as part of the appeal of fast food?

(A) It is cheap.   (B) It is high in calories.

TOEFL Vocabulary Practice

D. Fill in the blanks with the correct words.

negative	involve	attitudes	feature	insisting

1. Your research assignment will _____ an analysis of the literature, an experiment, and a summary of your findings.

2. The survey will assess consumer _____ toward corporate ethics with regards to the environment.

3. Failing to attend class will have a _____ impact on your final grade.

4. Lab work is an essential _____ of this class. It is worth fifteen percent of your grade.

5. I can't go camping with you this weekend. My boss is _____ that I work on Saturday.

Test

Read the passage.

Exercise

We all know that exercise is a good idea. It keeps the body healthy. It also helps to relieve stress. But there are different types of exercise. Some forms help you get strong. These are called strengthening exercises. Weight lifting is a good example. Other forms involve the heart and lungs. These are called aerobic exercises. Examples include jogging or riding a bike. Each type fulfills its own goals. Experts insist that people vary their exercise routines. Then they will get an adequate amount of each.

Strengthening exercises concentrate on muscles. Having strong muscles makes life easier. ■ 1) You can lift more things. You won't get hurt as easily. ■ 2) People with strong muscles have stronger bones. That means their bones do not break as easily. ■ 3) Weight lifting allows you to focus on certain body parts. You can work only the muscles that you want to improve. ■ 4) Finally, most people have the attitude that strong people are good looking.

Aerobic exercises feature repetitive movements. People workout by repeating the same movement at a fast pace. They will become out of breath. This is because their lungs are being worked. Their heart rates also increase. They start to sweat. This is because the body is warming up. That means that calories are being burned. People wanting to lose weight should do more aerobic exercise. Also, because of the different movements, coordination is improved.

A combination of the two types of exercise constitutes a healthy exercise program. It is the best way to keep your body at a healthy weight and looking its best. People who exercise each day tend to live a long life. This is especially true of people who do aerobic exercises. This is because their hearts and lungs get a workout too. They also say they enjoy life more.

Choose the correct answers.

1. The word forms in paragraph 2 is closest in meaning to

(A) kinds   (B) shape
(C) document   (D) mold

2. Look at the four squares [■] that indicate where the following sentence could be added to the passage.

So, if you want stronger arms, you can work out your arm muscles.

Where would the sentence best fit?

(A) Square 1   (B) Square 2
(C) Square 3   (D) Square 4

3. What can be inferred from paragraph 2?

(A) People with big muscles have more dating success.

(B) People with big muscles have more injuries.

4. According to the passage, which of the following is NOT mentioned as being part of aerobic exercises?

(A) increased heart rate

(B) focus on certain body part

5. Which of the following best expresses the essential information in the highlighted sentence? Incorrect answers change the meaning in important ways or leave out essential information.

A combination of the two types of exercise constitutes a healthy exercise program.

(A) Combining both types in a single workout is the best policy.

(B) Overall fitness is compromised by switching types.

6. Directions: An introductory sentence for a brief summary of the passage is provided below. Complete the summary by selecting the THREE answer choices that express the most important ideas in the passage. Some sentences do not belong in the summary because they express ideas that are not presented in the passage or are minor ideas in the passage.

People should get an adequate amount of the two main types of exercise to stay healthy and strong.

Answer choices

(A) Weight lifters are prone to accidents.

(B) Strengthening exercises are good for building muscles.

(C) They don't tend to be overweight.

(D) Aerobic exercises are good for your heart and lungs.

(E) A balanced combination of these two types of exercise constitutes a healthy program.

Check-up

A. Choose the correct answer.

1. What should you do when you come to a sentence simplification question?
   (A) Look for antonyms of words in the highlighted passage in the answer choices.
   (B) Look for synonyms of words in the highlighted passage in the answer choices.
   (C) Choose the answer that is longer than the highlighted passage.
   (D) Select the answer that contradicts the important points in the highlighted passage.

2. When you come to a sentence simplification question, you should
   (A) look for answer choices with the same sentence structure as the highlighted passage
   (B) choose the answer that leaves out the most important details of the highlighted passage
   (C) scan the answer choices for the sentence that uses the same words as the highlighted passage
   (D) select the answer that contains the most important details of the highlighted passage

Key Vocabulary Practice

B. Fill in the blanks with the correct words.

| immune system | disturbed | awake | popularity |
| well-being | overweight | calories | fast food |

1. AIDS is a condition that affects the _____, making it difficult to fight illness.
2. I am trying to lose some weight, so I am limiting the number of _____ I take in.
3. Meditation is a good way to relieve stress and improve your overall _____.
4. You should try to avoid eating _____.
5. Our study session was _____ by all of the noise on the streets.
6. Being _____ is unhealthy because it places a strain on your heart.
7. The _____ of the iPod means that they are hard to find because they sell out quickly.
8. My professor is so boring. I find it hard to stay _____ in class.

[10] Technology

Getting Ready to Read

A. Learn the words.

Key Vocabulary

film	a special material used to store images
load	to place into
wind	to return film to its plastic container
develop	to process; to make into a photograph

TOEFL Vocabulary

prior	before
digital	representing data or information as numbers
purchase	to buy
breakthrough	an important development
consumer	a person who buys things; a customer

B. Learn the question types.

TOEFL Question Types

Inference
What probably occurred after X?
Which of the following can be inferred from paragraph A about X?

- Scan the passage or paragraph specified for the information given in the question.
- Eliminate answer choices that are inaccurate or not mentioned in the passage.
- Ensure that your answer choice is logically supported by details in the passage.

Rhetorical Purpose
Why does the author compare X to Y?
Why does the author use the word X in discussing Y?
The author discusses X in paragraph 2 in order to...

- Familiarize yourself with the meanings of various purpose vocabulary used in these questions, such as the following: argue, classify, compare, contrast, criticize, emphasize, illustrate, persuade, summarize, etc.
- Carefully read for connections between the points raised in the question.
- Choose the answer that provides the most logical explanation for the author's writing.

C. Read the passage. Number each paragraph with the correct main idea or purpose.

1. Information on developing photos before the development of digital cameras
2. Information on taking photos before the development of digital cameras
3. Explanation of how digital cameras are different from film cameras
4. Explanation of how taking photos with a digital camera is different from taking photos with a film camera
5. Information on the popularity of digital cameras

Digital Cameras

___Prior to the introduction of digital cameras, taking photos was not easy. You had to purchase film. Then you had to load it into your camera. Then you could take your photos. But you couldn't see them yet.

___When you were finished with the film, you had to wind it up and take it out of the camera. Finally, you had to go to the store to have it developed. You had to pay for this service.

___Digital cameras were a breakthrough in technology. They do not store photos on film. They store them like a computer does.

___Photo-taking is now cheap and easy. People can see photos right away. They can see them on computers. It is easy to share photos through your email. You can also post them on websites.

___Most consumers prefer digital cameras. Film cameras are no longer common. Today, most photographers own a digital camera.

D. Complete the summary notes by filling in the blanks.

Topic:	Digital Cameras
In the past:	Before _____ cameras—purchase film, _____ it, take pictures.
	Couldn't _____ them.
Film cameras:	After taking pictures—wind up film, _____, and have _____.
Digital cameras:	Digital cameras _____ in _____.
	No film.
	Store photos like a _____.
Today:	Today—_____ and easy.
	_____ photos immediately.
	Put them on _____.
	Share via _____ and _____.
Conclusion:	_____ prefer digital to film.

E. Choose the correct answers.

1. Which of the following can be inferred from paragraph 4?

    (A) You shouldn't print photos from your computer.

    (B) You should have a computer if you buy a digital camera.

2. Which of the following can be inferred about film cameras?

    (A) They will soon be replaced.

    (B) They take better photos.

3. The author mentions winding film as an example of

    (A) a reason that film cameras are easier than digital cameras

    (B) a reason that digital cameras are easier than film cameras

4. Why does the author mention computers in paragraph 3?

    (A) To show that computers have changed the way we take pictures

    (B) To help explain how digital cameras are different from film cameras

TOEFL Vocabulary Practice

F. Fill in the blanks with the correct words.

prior	purchase	breakthrough	digital	consumers

1. _____ to the fall of the Berlin Wall, East Germany existed as a separate country.

2. The new product was not successful because _____ were unhappy with the change.

3. The introduction of _____ cameras has hurt companies that produce film.

4. I couldn't _____ a newspaper this morning because I had no money.

5. Scientists say the new vaccine is a _____ in the fight against the disease.

Practice

A. Learn the words.

Key Vocabulary

portable	easy to carry
memory	the capacity to store data
hard drive	an internal storage disk
album	a recording containing a collection of songs

TOEFL Vocabulary

primary	main; most significant
bulky	inconveniently large
collection	a group of things or people
acquire	to get; to obtain
multimedia	a system that incorporates sound, images, video, and text

Reading Passage

B. Read the passage and underline the key information.

iPods

The iPod has changed the way we listen to music. Today, it is the most popular portable music player. The primary reason for this is its memory. It can store thousands of songs. This is because it has a hard drive in it.

iPods are small and easy to carry. They are not as bulky as the older portable CD players. Again, they hold a lot more songs. CD players can only play one CD at a time. With an iPod, you can take your whole music collection with you wherever you go.

Music is easy to acquire with the iPod. You download music from the Internet. This is easier than going to the store and buying a CD. Plus, you can buy only the songs you like. You don't have to buy a whole album if you only like a few songs.

But music isn't the only thing iPods are good for. They are multimedia devices. You can store photos and even video on your iPod. There are games you can play on them, too. The Apple brand is now promoting the iPhone. It is an iPod that is also a mobile phone. It also has Internet access.

C. Choose the correct answers.

1. What can be inferred from paragraph 3?

    (A) iPods require you to download music illegally.

    (B) Purchasing music over the Internet lets you buy only the songs you want.

2. Why does the author mention the iPhone?

    (A) To show how the iPod is inferior

    (B) To show how the technology is expected to change

3. Which of the following best expresses the essential information in the highlighted sentence? Incorrect answers change the meaning in important ways or leave out essential information.

With the iPod, you can take your whole music collection with you wherever you go.

    (A) iPods allow you to take all your music with you.

    (B) iPods allow you to add new music from anywhere.

TOEFL Vocabulary Practice

D. Fill in the blanks with the correct words.

primary	acquire	multimedia	collections	bulky

1. I'm hoping to _____ some Aboriginal artwork for my new house.

2. My _____ role is as an educator. My research comes second to teaching.

3. My old printer was quite _____ but my new one is much smaller.

4. Teachers are increasingly utilizing _____ devices to appeal to different learning styles.

5. The Vatican has one of the most valuable art _____ in the world.

Read the passage.

Printing

Prior to the invention of the printing press, it was very difficult to print a book. You had to carve the letters into wood, stone, or metal. Next, you had to apply ink. Then, you could stamp the image onto paper. To print the next page, you had to do it all over again. So, books were rare. ■ **1)** The finished product was different, too. ■ **2)** People made the page look nice to make it worth all of the effort. ■ **3)** There were many designs and pictures on the earliest printed material. ■ **4)**

In 1450, there was a major breakthrough. Johann Gutenberg invented a printing press. This might be the most important invention to date. Its primary purpose was to make printing cheap. It did this through the use of movable type. Separate blocks were created for each letter. The letters could be easily arranged. Printing became cheaper. Books could be purchased in order to acquire information. This opened up the world of science, arts, and religion to the average consumer.

Since then, printing has become cheaper and easier. In the nineteenth century, the "linotype" was invented. You didn't have to arrange the letters by hand. You could press keys to arrange them. It was like a typewriter. This reduced the number of people needed to operate the printing machine.

The last century saw many advances in printing technology. Computers are popular multi-media devices where users can store their music and video collections on their hard drives. They are now also the primary method of creating text. It is easy to enter text into your computer. Then you can send it to your printer. Today's printers are less bulky, and more portable, than the old printing presses. In seconds, you have a printed page. Digital presses are being used for very large printing jobs.

Choose the correct answers.

1. Look at the four squares [■] that indicate where the following sentence could be added to the passage.

   That made it expensive.

   Where would the sentence best fit?
   (A) Square 1   (B) Square 2
   (C) Square 3   (D) Square 4

2. According to the passage, which of the following was NOT mentioned as part of the impact of Gutenberg's printing press?

(A) Printing became cheaper.

(B) It opened up the world of science, arts, and religion to the average consumer.

(C) Printed work stopped featuring decorations.

(D) More people could acquire information.

3. The word it in paragraph 2 refers to

(A) the computer

(B) the keys

(C) the text

(D) the printing press

4. What can be inferred about Gutenberg's press from paragraph 3?

(A) It was expensive.

(B) It broke easily.

(C) It is no longer the best printing option.

(D) It replaced skilled workers with unskilled.

5. Which of the following best expresses the essential information in the highlighted sentence? Incorrect answers change the meaning in important ways or leave out essential information.

This reduced the number of people needed to operate the printing machine.

(A) The printing machine required fewer operators.

(B) Fewer printing machines were needed to print large works.

(C) Having less people working saved money in printing.

(D) This created demand for unskilled workers.

6. Directions: An introductory sentence for a brief summary of the passage is provided below. Complete the summary by selecting the THREE answer choices that express the most important ideas in the passage. Some sentences do not belong in the summary because they express ideas that are not presented in the passage or are minor ideas in the passage.

Printing technology has changed a great deal over the years.

Answer choices

(A) The first printed work was time consuming and expensive.

(B) Johann Gutenberg was a famous printer.

(C) Johann Gutenberg invented the printing press, which made printing cheap and easy.

(D) Technology has continued and continues to improve the efficiency of printing.

(E) Today, the science of printing has been perfected.

Check-up

A. Choose the correct answers.

1. What should you do when you come to an inference question?
    (A) Ensure your answer choice contains the specific information given in the question.
    (B) Select the answer choice that is logically supported by details in the passage.
    (C) Ensure your answer choice contradicts the information given in the passage.
    (D) Select the answer choice that best expresses the main idea of the passage.

2. When you come to a rhetorical purpose question, you should
    (A) choose the answer choice that best suggests what will occur next
    (B) select the answer choice that contains a synonym for the word mentioned in the question
    (C) scan the passage for synonyms of the word mentioned in the question
    (D) ensure your answer provides the most logical explanation for the author's writing

Key Vocabulary Practice

B. Fill in the blanks with the correct words.

film	load	wind	developed
portable	memory	hard drive	album

1. My computer can't handle this program. I'm going to need some more
    _____.

2. I have to pick up my photos from my vacation. I had them _____ at the camera store at the mall.

3. We need to _____ the fridge with beverages for the barbecue.

4. If there's a problem with the _____, you should get a professional to open up the computer.

5. We need to get _____ for the camera. I want to get lots of photos.

6. I got a new _____ DVD player. Now I can watch whatever movie I want on the plane.

7. Don't _____ it yet! There are still ten more photos on the roll.

8. My favorite band is putting out a new _____ next week. I can't wait to hear it.

[11] Civics and Government

Getting Ready to Read

A. Learn the words.

Key Vocabulary

rule	to govern; to control
dictator	a ruler with unlimited power
practice	to do something as an established custom or habit
citizen	a recognized member of a political society

TOEFL Vocabulary

democracy	a system of government in which the people effectively hold the power
originate	to begin; to start
govern	to rule over; to control
authority	the right to command or make decisions
assembly	a gathering; the coming together of people for a peaceful purpose

B. Learn the question type.

TOEFL Question Type

Insert Text

Look at the four squares [■] that indicate where the following sentence could be added to the passage.

[You will see a sentence in bold.]

Where would the sentence best fit?

- Try inserting the sentence into each place marked by a square [■], and eliminate any that are obviously incorrect.
- Look for logical connections in content between the sentence given and the sentences before and after each square.
- Look for structural connections, like pronouns and referents, parallel grammatical structure, or transitional words and phrases.
- Choose the position that makes the most logical and structural sense with the rest of the passage.

C. Read the passage. Number each paragraph with the correct main idea or purpose.

> 1. Explanation of what a democracy is not
> 2. Information on a modern democracy
> 3. Information on the beginnings and a definition of democracy
> 4. Information on the first democracy

Democracy

___ ■ **1)** Democracy originated a long time ago in ancient Greece. ■ **2)** It means rule by the people. ■ **3)** In a democracy, the people are governed by the people. ■ **4)** ___In a true democracy, there is no single person that holds all of the power. ■ **5)** In other words, the people are not governed by a dictator. ■ **6)** A dictator is someone who has the authority to rule over all of the people. ■ **7)** Dictators only look out for themselves. ■ **8)**

___The ancient Greeks practiced direct democracy. That meant that all citizens could take part in government. They could attend assemblies and vote. However, slaves and women were not considered citizens. They could not take part.

___Today, we elect people to speak for us. We vote for the person who we think expresses our interests best. The person with the most votes wins. He or she will then represent the voters. In this way, the people can participate in government.

D. Complete the summary notes by filling in the blanks.

Topic: Democracy
Introduction: _____ in ancient Greece.
                Rule by the _____.
Details: No _____—no one with _____ to rule over
                everyone.
Ancient Greece: Ancient Greeks—practiced _____ democracy.
                All _____ could take part.
                _____ and _____ not citizens.
Today: Today—_____ representatives.
                They _____ voters.

E. Choose the correct answers.

1. Look at the four squares [■] that indicate where the following sentence could be added to the passage.

That's where the word comes from.

Where would the sentence best fit?
(A) Square 1
(B) Square 2
(C) Square 3
(D) Square 4

2. Look at the four squares [■] that indicate where the following sentence could be added to the passage.

They don't care about the common good.

Where would the sentence best fit?
(A) Square 5
(B) Square 6
(C) Square 7
(D) Square 8

TOEFL Vocabulary Practice

F. Fill in the blanks with the correct words.

democracy	originated	governed	authority	assembly

1. We are _____ by elected officials, not a king or a queen.

2. A good teacher must establish _____ without appearing as the enemy.

3. The disease _____ in birds, but it can be spread to the humans who handle them.

4. The principal announced that the _____ would begin at three o'clock.

5. The founding fathers of the United States created the first modern _____.

Practice

A. Learn the words.

Key Vocabulary

executive	the decision-making section of government
cabinet	a body of government officials who advise the President
Supreme Court	the highest court in the US
judicial	relating to court judgments

TOEFL Vocabulary

individual	one person
function	a purpose; what something is used for
legislation	a law; the process of making laws
Congress	the US government body that makes laws
branch	a division of a larger organization

Reading Passage

B. Read the passage and underline the key information.

Three Branches of Government

The founders of the United States wanted to form a new kind of government. ■ **1)** Most had come from Britain and other places in Europe. They were used to having a king or queen. ■ **2)** They did not want this for their new country. They did not want any individual to have too much power over the citizens of the country. ■ **3)** That's why they set up a government with three branches of government. Each of the branches has a different function. ■ **4)**

One of the branches is in charge of making legislation. That means that it makes the laws of the country. It is made up of Congress and other groups. Members of Congress are elected.

The executive branch makes sure that the laws are followed. It consists of the president, the vice-president, and the cabinet. Cabinet members are chosen by the president. They give him or her advice.

The judicial branch decides what the laws mean. Sometimes, people disagree on how to read laws. When this issue comes up, the Supreme Court decides.

The power of each branch is limited. This keeps each group from becoming too powerful. Each branch can change decisions made by other branches. This maintains the balance of power.

C. Choose the correct answers.

1. Look at the four squares [■] that indicate where the following sentence could be added to the passage.

They also have their own limited powers.

Where would the sentence best fit?

(A) Square 1   (B) Square 2
(C) Square 3   (D) Square 4

2. Which of the following can be inferred from paragraph 1?

(A) A US president had more power than a British king or queen.
(B) A US president had less power than a British king or queen.

3. Why does the author mention kings and queens?

(A) To contrast their powers with one another
(B) To contrast the powers of a monarch with the powers of a president

TOEFL Vocabulary Practice

D. Fill in the blanks with the correct words.

individual	function	legislation	Congress	branches

1. Some of the larger banks have _____ all over the world.

2. The _____ of the lab assistant is to help you with the equipment.

3. The president vetoed the _____, forcing law makers to compromise in order to pass the bill.

4. The rights of the _____ must be protected from majority rule.

5. Elections for the US _____ are held every two years.

Read the passage.

The Bill of Rights

Freedom is very important in the United States. The country was started by people from Europe. Some originated in countries with little freedom. They came to America for this reason. They wanted to create a country where people were free. So, they started a democracy. They did not want to be governed by a dictator.

Democracy is based on majority rule. Issues are decided this way. If most people think it should be one way, then that's how it will be. The founding fathers were very wise. They saw that majority rule might harm individuals. They wanted to protect each citizen. They decided to limit the power of the government. They did this by creating the Bill of Rights. The function of this bill was to set rights and freedoms. No one has the authority to take them away. It is the job of the Supreme Court to make sure no one does so.

The Bill of Rights says that citizens can practice their religion. People are free to speak out against the government. They are also free to gather together as long as they are peaceful. The press is allowed to operate no matter what. People in the US also have the right to have a gun. Congress may not pass legislation that denies these rights.

Other rights have to do with criminal law. For example, suspected criminals have the right to a fair trial. It must be quick and open to others. They can choose to have a jury. ■ 1) A jury is a group of people who are not experts in the law. ■ 2) They decide if a person is guilty or not guilty. ■ 3) Criminals have the right not to be punished unfairly. ■ 4) Punishment cannot be cruel or unusual. These are just some of the rights guaranteed to American citizens.

Choose the correct answers.

1. The word free in paragraph 1 is closest in meaning to
   (A) available   (B) costless
   (C) at large   (D) liberated

2. According to the passage, what was the main purpose of the Bill of Rights?
   (A) To protect individuals against the whims of the majority
   (B) To ensure that there would never be a dictator
   (C) To establish the power of the Supreme Court
   (D) To establish independence from Britain

3. What can be inferred from paragraph 2 about majority rule?

(A) It creates the greatest good for the greatest number of people.
(B) It is the one drawback of a democracy.
(C) It can tend to be oppressive to members of the minority.
(D) It relies on having an educated population.

4. Which of the following best expresses the essential information in the highlighted sentence? Incorrect answers change the meaning in important ways or leave out essential information.

They are also free to gather together as long as they are peaceful.

(A) Gatherings are not allowed during wartime.
(B) Assemblies in the name of peace are permitted.
(C) They can gather as long as they do not protest violently.
(D) They have the right to protest peacefully, too.

5. Look at the four squares [■] that indicate where the following sentence could be added to the passage.

They are considered the peers of the defendant.

Where would the sentence best fit?

(A) Square 1   (B) Square 2
(C) Square 3   (D) Square 4

6. Directions: An introductory sentence for a brief summary of the passage is provided below. Complete the summary by selecting the THREE answer choices that express the most important ideas in the passage. Some sentences do not belong in the summary because they express ideas that are not presented in the passage or are minor ideas in the passage.

The Bill of Rights establishes certain rights to US Citizens.

Answer choices

(A) The founding fathers did not want individuals to be harmed by those in power.
(B) So, they wrote the Bill of Rights to expand the power of the majority.
(C) So, they wrote the Bill of Rights to limit the power of the government.
(D) This led to the establishment of rights for criminals.
(E) This established several basic rights that all individuals in the US should have.

Check-up

A. Choose the correct answers.

1. What should you do when you come to an insert text question?
   (A) Look for details in the sentence given that repeat in the sentence after each square.
   (B) Choose the position with the strongest structural connections between the sentence given and the sentences before and after it.
   (C) Look for the essential details from the sentence given in the sentence before each square.
   (D) Choose the position in which the given sentence best contradicts the logic and structure of the sentences before and after it.

Key Vocabulary Practice

B. Fill in the blanks with the correct words.

dictator	citizen	ruled	practice
executive	judicial	cabinet	Supreme Court

1. My grandfather lived in the US for many years before becoming a _____.

2. They were ruled by a ruthless _____ for many years before they revolted.

3. The president made the decision based on the advice of his _____.

4. The protester wished to _____ his right to free speech.

5. The US President is in charge of the _____ branch of government.

6. The _____ overruled the original ruling, declaring it unconstitutional.

7. Some countries, such as Saudi Arabia, are still _____ by a king.

8. The Supreme Court belongs to the _____ branch of government.

[12] Communication

Getting Ready to Read

A. Learn the words.

Key Vocabulary

communication	the ways people tell each other information
expression	revelation of one's thoughts or feelings through actions
body language	body posture and facial expressions that can be used to express feelings or emotions
frown	an angry or worried look

TOEFL Vocabulary

verbal	relating to spoken words
nonverbal	relating to unspoken communication; not involving words
gesture	an action, usually with arms and/or hands
confident	being sure of yourself and your ideas/opinions
contact	interaction; connection

B. Learn the question type.

TOEFL Question Type

Table

Directions: Complete the table below by matching the X below.

Directions: Select the appropriate X from the answer choices and match them to Y. TWO of the answer choices will not be used. This question is worth 3/4 points.

- Eliminate any answer choices that obviously do not relate to any of the table categories.
- Scan the passage for the details given in the remaining answer choices and look for logical or structural connections to one of the table categories.
- Some points are awarded for having at least half of the answers correct, so fill in all the spaces in the table, even if you are unsure of the answers.

C. Read the passage. Number each paragraph with the correct main idea or purpose.

> 1. Positive body language
> 2. Non-verbal communication
> 3. Verbal communication
> 4. Negative body language

Body Language

___People use two kinds of communication. Verbal communication is done by talking. It is what we say to each other. It uses words.

___Non-verbal communication uses the body. It is what we show each other. It uses gestures and facial expressions. That is why it is called body language. It makes up fifty-five percent of communication. People should learn to read body language. It helps to understand what people really want to say.

___There are many examples of positive body language. Positive body language sends a happy message. People look friendly if they smile. They look confident when they stand straight. They get attention by making eye contact.

___Negative body language sends a bad message. It tells people to go away. It tells people to be scared. Crossing arms makes people look angry. Frowning makes people look worried. Looking down makes people look shy. Looking away makes people look bored.

D. Complete the summary notes by filling in the blanks.

Topic:	Body Language
Communication:	_____ kinds—verbal and _____.
Verbal:	Uses _____.
Non-verbal:	Uses _____ and facial _____.
	Also called body _____.
	Makes up _____ percent of communication.
Positive body language:	Sends _____ messages.
Examples:	Smiles look _____.
	Standing straight looks _____.
	Making eye contact gets _____.
Negative body language:	Sends _____ messages.
Examples:	Crossing arms looks _____.
	_____ looks worried.
	Looking down looks _____.
	Looking away looks _____.

E. Choose the correct answers.

1. Complete the table by matching the phrases below with the type of communication they represent. TWO of the answer choices will NOT be used.

Answer choices

(A) Uses gestures and facial expressions
(B) Look confident
(C) Communication by talking
(D) Uses words
(E) Used by deaf people
(F) Makes up fifty-five percent of communication
(G) Shown with the body

Verbal communication

- _____
- _____

Nonverbal communication

- _____
- _____
- _____

2. Complete the table by matching the examples below with the type of body language they represent. TWO of the answer choices will NOT be used.

Answer choices

(A) Crossing arms   (B) Smiling
(C) Looking away   (D) Dancing
(E) Making eye contact   (F) Frowning
(G) Looking down   (H) Standing straight
(I) Clapping

Positive body language

- _____
- _____
- _____

Negative body language

- _____
- _____
- _____
- _____

TOEFL Vocabulary Practice

F. Fill in the blanks with the correct words.

nonverbal	gestures	verbal	confident	contact

1. Instead of speaking, most deaf people use hand _____.

2. Frowning is an example of _____ communication.

3. Hitler was _____ that he would win the war.

4. Scientists would like to make _____ with intelligent life in space.

5. The law does not always recognize _____ agreements.

Practice

A. Learn the words.

Key Vocabulary

stutter	to say or speak with difficulty, by stopping and starting several times
impediment	an impairment or obstacle
hard time	difficulty
avoid	to try not to do or be near

TOEFL Vocabulary

perceive	to get an idea by using one's senses
awkward	clumsy; without style or grace
concentration	the condition of having a focused mind
public speaking	speaking before a large group of people
speech	a public address

Reading Passage

B. Read the passage and underline the key information.

Stuttering

Stuttering is a kind of speech impediment. It is when you have a hard time getting words out. It means that sometimes you repeat some sounds, and sometimes you cannot finish saying words. Stuttering often starts when you are a child. People who stutter try to avoid saying words that make them stutter. They also try to avoid speaking in front of other people.

■ 1) People who stutter feel nervous when they talk to people. ■ 2) They feel shy about how slowly they speak. ■ 3) They think that other people will perceive them as stupid because they speak slowly and awkwardly. ■ 4)

To help a person that stutters you should speak slowly and clearly yourself. You should also wait a few seconds to ensure they have finished talking before you reply. Do not finish their sentences and do not rush them. This just makes the person lose concentration. Losing one's concentration can make stuttering worse.

Public speaking is also very hard for stutterers. Winston Churchill is a famous public speaker who stuttered. He had to make many speeches. He worked very hard to stop stuttering.

In fact, many famous people stutter. The American golfer, Tiger Woods, stuttered as a child. So did Julia Roberts.

C. Choose the correct answers.

1. Complete the table below by matching the appropriate phrases and words from the answer choices and matching them to the feelings and behavior of people who stutter. TWO of the answer choices will NOT be used.
This question is worth 3 points.

Answer choices

(A) Nervous
(B) Saying words that make them stutter
(C) Stupid
(D) Confident
(E) Public speaking
(F) Shy
(G) Singing

They avoid

• _____
• _____

They feel

• _____
• _____
• _____

2. Look at the four squares [■] that indicate where the following sentence could be added to the passage.

The truth is that stuttering does not make you stupid.

Where would the sentence best fit?

(A) Square 1   (B) Square 2
(C) Square 3   (D) Square 4

TOEFL Vocabulary Practice

D. Fill in the blanks with the correct words.

perceived	public speaking	awkward	concentrate	speech

1. During one's teenage years, it is common to feel _____ and shy.

2. Humans need enough sleep to _____ on their work.

3. John F. Kennedy made a famous _____ at the Berlin Wall in the 1960s.

4. Writer Oscar Wilde enjoyed being _____ as a great wit.

5. Many schools have _____ contests for students.

Test

Read the passage.

Public Speaking

Public speaking is an art, but it is something that anyone can learn to be good at. We can all learn to speak well in front of others by following a few rules.

If you want to be a good public speaker, it helps to feel confident. That means being sure of what it is you are speaking about. You should study your subject before you begin. You should also practice your speech at home a few times. It helps to make small speech cards. Write key words on these cards. These words will help you remember what you want to say.

Everyone feels nervous when they have to speak in front of others. It is natural to feel nervous. If you look confident, however, people will perceive you as confident. Even if you feel very awkward on the inside, you can hide it. Stand up straight, breathe slowly, and don't lose your concentration. Just focus on the main ideas of your speech. Make sure you smile, make eye contact, and don't frown! Try to make your gestures natural.

You should also try not to speak too quickly. It takes time for people to understand new ideas. Remember that you are trying to communicate your ideas. Slow down and break up difficult ideas into shorter sentences. Speeches are very much like essays. They have a beginning, middle, and end.

Speak as loudly and clearly as you can. ■ 1) This will help you to keep your listener's attention. ■ 2) Avoid using big words that you don't understand. ■ 3) If you don't understand your own speech, no one else will! ■ 4)

Start your speech with a strong statement. This will make people listen. In your conclusion, it helps to repeat your main ideas. If you use these helpful hints, you will become a better public speaker.

Choose the correct answers.

1. The word confident in the passage is closest in meaning to

   (A) withdrawn
   (B) self-assured
   (C) unhappy
   (D) excited

2. According to the passage, all of the following are required to make a good speech EXCEPT

   (A) make speech cards
   (B) practice your speech at home
   (C) write key words on your hands
   (D) study the subject of your speech

3. What can be inferred about looking confident during a speech from paragraph 3?

(A) You can never hide feeling nervous.
(B) Positive body language helps you look confident.
(C) Confidence exercises should be practiced daily.
(D) Confidence problems only affect some people.

4. Look at the four squares [■] that indicate where the following sentence could be added to the passage.

If speech is too soft or unclear, people get bored.

Where would the sentence best fit?

(A) Square 1
(C) Square 3
(B) Square 2
(D) Square 4

5. Which of the following best expresses the essential information in the highlighted sentence? Incorrect answers change the meaning in important ways or leave out essential information.

In your conclusion, it helps to repeat your main ideas.

(A) Your conclusion should have ideas that help listeners.
(B) It is a good idea to re-state key thoughts at the end of a speech.
(C) Repeating your opinions during a speech will bore your listeners.
(D) In conclusion, speechmakers mainly use important ideas to aid them.

6. Directions: Complete the table below by matching the appropriate phrases to what should or should not be done in public speaking. TWO of the answer choices will NOT be used. This question is worth 4 points.

Answer choices

(A) Use big words
(B) Practice your speech
(C) Do mouth stretching exercises
(D) Speak softly
(E) Drink water before speaking
(F) Study your subject
(G) Make cards with key words
(H) Stand straight
(I) Speak quickly

Should do in public speaking
• _____
• _____
• _____
• _____

Shouldn't do in public speaking
• _____
• _____
• _____

Check-up

A. Choose the correct answer.

1. When you come to a table completion question, you should
   (A) sort the answer choices according to logical connections to the categories
   (B) leave sections of the table empty if your are unsure of the answers
   (C) ensure you put all of the answer choices into the table
   (D) choose the answer choice that best summarizes the main idea of the passage

Key Vocabulary Practice

B. Fill in the blanks with the correct words.

avoid	expression	communication	body language
stutter	frown	hard time	impediment

1. Children who _____ can often be helped by a speech therapist.

2. Smoking is an _____ to good health.

3. A smile is an _____ of joy or friendliness.

4. If you have a _____ with your car, you should visit a mechanic.

5. People who suffer from stomach problems should _____ acidic foods.

6. A good detective can tell if you are lying by observing your _____.

7. The cell phone is a very convenient form of _____.

8. People who _____ too much will get many wrinkles.

[Review 2]

Read the passage.

Health

Many schools have campaigns to get students to eat healthy foods. Schools fund these programs because a lot of people think that kids eat too much junk food. Junk foods have a lot of calories. The more calories food has, the more energy it can give us. We rely on calories for energy. It is not good if we consume too many calories. It could make us fat.

People need a certain number of calories per day. We need these calories for energy. We need energy for things like walking, running, working, and concentrating. ■ 1) If we eat more calories than we need, we can become fat. ■ 2) If we don't eat an adequate amount of calories, we may lose weight. ■ 3) If we lose too much weight, it could have a negative effect on our health. ■ 4)

We also have to concentrate on what kind of calories we eat. Some calories have energy, but they are not healthy for us. They do not feature the vitamins that our bodies need. These calories are called "empty calories." Candy, soda and other foods with sugar have empty calories. These foods are not very good for us.

It is OK to eat these empty calories sometimes. However, we must remember to vary the food that we eat. This will give us a healthy diet. A diet with the right amount of good calories will make us healthy and strong. It will make our coordination better and help us get through the day.

Choose the correct answers.

1. The phrase junk food in the passage is closest in meaning to

(A) vitamins
(B) unhealthy food
(C) empty calories
(D) garbage

2. According to the author, empty calories are not good for us because

(A) they have too much energy
(B) they don't have enough energy
(C) they don't have enough vitamins
(D) they can make us sick

3. According to the passage, which of the following is NOT true of calories?

    (A) A calorie is a unit of food energy.
    (B) There is more than one type of calorie.
    (C) Empty calories are the best kind to eat.
    (D) Too many calories can make people fat.

4. Which of the following best expresses the essential information in the highlighted sentence? Incorrect answers change the meaning in important ways or leave out essential information.

    People need a certain number of calories per day.

    (A) People should eat a random amount of calories each day.
    (B) People need to consume empty calories every day.
    (C) People need to eat the right amount of calories every day.
    (D) People need to eat vitamins every day.

5. Which of the following can be inferred about calories?

    (A) They play an important part in our health.
    (B) Only adults need to worry about calories.
    (C) Calories and vitamins are the same thing.
    (D) You should only eat empty calories.

6. Look at the four squares [■] that indicate where the following sentence could be added to the passage.

    That's why it is important to eat the right amount of calories.

    Where would the sentence best fit?

    (A) Square 1   (B) Square 2
    (C) Square 3   (D) Square 4

Choose the correct answers.

The Magna Carta

The Magna Carta is a document that was written in England in 1215. The Magna Carta means "Great Charter" or "Great Paper." Some people think it is one of the most important papers in the history of democracy. ■ **1)** It is where many of today's laws come from. ■ **2)** These laws were important. ■ **3)** They were laws that protected the individual. ■ **4)**

The Magna Carta was a new approach to how a king ruled his subjects. There were disagreements over how a king should govern. That is why The Magna Carta was written. People realized that everyone should have rights. They wanted to limit the king's authority. The Magna Carta demonstrated a change in attitudes. The philosophy of ruling at the time was that the king could do anything he wanted. These new attitudes led to The Magna Carta.

The Magna Carta stated that all people have certain rights. One was the right not to be put into jail for no reason. We still have that right today. The laws were not only for rich people. The laws were for those in poverty, too. One function of The Magna Carta was to make the law equal for all people.

The Magna Carta is not a single document. The Magna Carta constitutes a set of documents. Together, they have a single name. The Magna Carta was first introduced in 1215. It was rewritten many times. The changes went on through the sixteenth and seventeenth centuries.

Most of The Magna Carta has been changed. Many of the ideas still live on, however. Many ideas in the US Constitution originated with The Magna Carta. The Magna Carta is one of the most important papers in history. It still affects our lives today.

Choose the correct answers.

1. The word document in paragraph 1 is closest in meaning to

(A) a formal piece of writing   (B) a book

(C) a rule   (D) a law

2. The word they in paragraph 4 refers to

(A) laws   (B) people

(C) kings   (D) documents

3. According to the passage, The Magna Carta was written because

(A) the king wanted the people to have more power
(B) the king wanted the people to have less power
(C) the people wanted the king to have more power
(D) the people wanted the king to have less power

4. Which of the following best expresses the essential information in the highlighted sentence? Incorrect answers change the meaning in important ways or leave out essential information.

The Magna Carta stated that all people have certain rights.

(A) Only rich people have rights and freedoms.
(B) Only poor people have rights and freedoms.
(C) Every person, rich or poor, has rights.
(D) Only the king has rights.

5. Look at the four squares [■] that indicate where the following sentence could be added to the passage.

Laws that protect the individual are still important today.

Where would the sentence best fit?

(A) Square 1   (B) Square 2
(C) Square 3   (D) Square 4

6. Why does the author mention the US Constitution?

(A) To show how it influenced The Magna Carta
(B) To show how The Magna Carta affects us today
(C) To show why The Magna Carta was written
(D) To explain why the US does not have a king

Read the passage.

How Technology Changed Our Phones

There have been many recent breakthroughs in technology. Now consumers can purchase the latest high tech toys. This was not possible even a few years ago. We don't have to carry our bulky CD players around anymore. Now, we can carry our whole music collection with us.

We can carry all of our music on our phones. That's right, our phones. A phone isn't just a phone anymore. Its primary purpose is to make and take calls. But now a phone is a multimedia center, too. We can play music, surf the Net, and even take pictures. It used to be that phones, record players, and cameras were all different things. Now they are one and the same. More tools get added to phones every day. Sometimes a phone is two different tools. Sometimes it is even three different tools.

There are many different options for phones these days. Sometimes a phone is also a camera. Other times it is an MP3 player. In some cases, it is a personal planner. It can also be a mini-computer. Sometimes a phone is all of these things put together.

The introduction of MP3 computer files was very important. It made it possible for us to store music in digital format. This means that there is no album or disc. We can acquire music by going onto the Internet and downloading it. We can download our favorite songs right onto our phones. We can use the cameras in our phone to take pictures. Then we can email the pictures to friends. We can do all of this with our phones.

Technology has led to a shift in how we do things. Prior to this, our high tech phones were not possible. We could only dream about the phones of today.

1. According to the passage, the new high tech devices are available because of
   (A) cheaper prices
   (B) demand
   (C) the Internet
   (D) breakthroughs in technology

2. The word it in paragraph 4 refers to
   (A) a cell phone
   (B) an MP3 player
   (C) a camera
   (D) music

3. The author's description of cell phones mentions all of the following EXCEPT

    (A) televisions
    (B) cameras
    (C) MP3 players
    (D) mini-computers

4. Which of the following can be inferred about MP3 files?

    (A) They are expensive.
    (B) They sound better than CDs.
    (C) They can be bought in more places.
    (D) They made cell phone cameras possible.

5. The author discusses different options for phones in paragraph 3 in order to

    (A) show how advanced the new phones are
    (B) explain how phones work
    (C) show how advanced cameras are
    (D) explain how MP3 players work

6. Complete the table below about the uses of phones discussed in the passage. Match the phrases to the column that best describes their use. TWO of the answer choices will NOT be used. This question is worth 3 points.

Answer choices

(A) Watch TV
(B) Listen to music
(C) Make calls
(D) Receive calls
(E) Take pictures
(F) Word processing
(G) Personal planner

Primary use of phone
- _____
- _____

Optional use of phone
- _____
- _____
- _____

Reading 2
Answer Key

Answer Key

[Unit 1]

Getting Ready

Page 14

C

3, 1, 4, 5, 2

D

Topic:	William Shakespeare
Introduction:	Lived in England from 1564–<u>1616</u>.
	One of world's <u>best writers</u>.
	Life divided into <u>three periods</u>.
Period 1:	First <u>twenty</u> years spent in Stratford.
	Early part of his life often called the <u>dark years</u> because there are no <u>records</u> of it.
Period 2:	Second part in the <u>theater</u>.
	Worked as an <u>actor</u> in London.
	Wrote many <u>plays</u> over twenty-five years.
Period 3:	<u>Retirement</u> spent in Stratford.
	Lived off money from <u>his earlier work</u>.

Page 15

E

1. B   2. A   3. A   4. B

F

1. period   2. records   3. divided
4. retirement   5. completed

Practice

Page 17

C

1. A   2. B   3. B   4. B

D

1. royal   2. empire   3. class
4. religious   5. explored

Test

Pages 18–19

1. C   2. B   3. C   4. D
5. C   6. A, C, E

Check-up

Page 20

A

1. C   2. B

B

1. priest   2. actor   3. live off
4. writer   5. carvings   6. covered
7. play   8. Researchers

[Unit 2]

Getting Ready

Page 22

C

3, 5, 1, 2, 4

D

Topic:	Frank Lloyd Wright
Introduction:	Wright is a <u>famous</u> American <u>architect</u>.
Training:	Went to university in <u>Wisconsin</u>, but didn't <u>graduate</u>.
	Also trained with a <u>construction</u> company.
Chicago:	Designed homes that <u>suited the city</u>.
	This time called his <u>Prairie</u> Period.
	No company would <u>hire</u> him because they thought he had no <u>morals</u>, so he <u>left the country</u>.
Europe:	Encouraged several <u>architectural</u> traditions by publishing a <u>book</u> of pictures of his <u>houses</u>.
Return to US:	Returned to the <u>US</u>, and designed buildings to <u>suit</u> the world around them. <u>Falling Water</u> is the most famous of these.

Page 23

E

1. A   2. B   3. A   4. B

F

1. defined   2. architect   3. traditions
4. designed   5. construction

Practice

Page 25

C

1. A   2. A   3. B   4. A

D

1. technique   2. debate   3. element
4. civilization   5. constraints

Test

Pages 26–27

1. A   2. C   3. A   4. C
5. D   6. B, C, E

Check-up

Page 28

A

1. B   2. A

B

1. hire   2. spire   3. stories
4. moral   5. suited   6. influential
7. impractical   8. antenna

[Unit 3]

Getting Ready

Page 30

C

3, 2, 1, 4, 5

D

Topic:	Plant Development
Introduction:	Study of plant development called <u>botany</u>.
	Plants begin as <u>seeds</u>.
	<u>Roots</u> grow downward from seeds.
Roots:	Roots grow in <u>soil or water</u>.
	They provide plants with <u>nutrients</u> and water.
	They hold plant in the <u>ground</u>.
Stem:	Stems develop upward from <u>seeds</u>.
	They keep plant leaves away from some <u>insects and animals</u>.
	They bring nutrients from the <u>roots</u> to the <u>leaves</u>.
Leaves:	Leaves make <u>food</u> from sunlight, CO_2, and water.
	The food is <u>sugar</u> and <u>oxygen</u>.
Seeds:	Plants must be <u>pollinated</u> to make seeds.
	Colorful, nice-smelling <u>flowers</u> attract pollinators to distribute <u>pollen</u>.

Page 31

E

1. A   2. B

F

1. investigation   2. botany   3. distributed
4. absorbs   5. established

Practice

Page 33

C

1. B   2. B   3. A

D

1. obtained   2. maintenance   3. emerged
4. regions   5. distinct

Answer Key

Test

Pages 34–35

1. D   2. D   3. D   4. B
5. D   6. A, D, E

Check-up

Page 36

A

1. C   2. B

B

1. corpse   2. Nutrients   3. germinate
4. nickname   5. cultivation   6. deforestation
7. development   8. pollinate

[Unit 4]

Getting Ready

Page 38

C

3, 5, 2, 1, 4

D

Topic:	The Atom
Size:	Grain of sand has <u>a lot of</u> atoms.
Importance:	Atoms are <u>the foundation</u> of all things.
Parts:	Atom has <u>three</u> parts.
	<u>Protons</u> have a positive charge.
	<u>Neutrons</u> have a neutral charge.
	<u>Electrons</u> have a negative charge.
Identification:	The number of <u>protons</u> specifies what an atom is.
	Number of protons is called the <u>atomic number</u>.
Core:	The core has <u>protons</u> and <u>neutrons</u>.
	Electrons <u>orbit</u> around core.

Page 39

E

1. A   2. A   3. A   4. B

F

1. dense   2. atom   3. approximately
4. specifies   5. foundation

Practice

Page 41

C

1. A   2. B   3. A

D

1. invisible   2. react   3. occur
4. associated   5. reaction

Test

Pages 42–43

1. A   2. D   3. B   4. D
5. C   6. B, C, E

Check-up

Page 44

A

1. C   2. A

B

1. positive charge   2. bubbles   3. grains
4. laboratories   5. atomic   6. weak
7. dissolve   8. negative charge

[Unit 5]

Getting Ready

Page 46

C

3, 2, 1. 4

D

Topic:	Seasonal Businesses
Introduction:	Makes <u>money</u> at certain times of year.

All year:	Some stay <u>open</u> all year.
	Make most money in one <u>season</u>.
	Try to <u>boost</u> sales in <u>off-season</u>.
Off-season:	Some close <u>during</u> off-season.
	Doesn't <u>make sense</u> to stay open.
	Not worth the <u>expense</u>.
Staff:	Summer businesses—<u>employ</u> students.
	Winter businesses—hard to find <u>staff</u>.

Page 47

E

1. D   2. C

F

1. employ   2. typical   3. expenses
4. staff   5. seasonal

Practice

Page 49

C

1. B   2. A   3. B

D

1. budget   2. competitor   3. persuade
4. alternatively 5. finances

Test

Pages 50–51

1. D   2. A   3. C   4. B
5. A   6. A, C, D

Check-up

Page 52

A

1. D

B

1. off-season   2. stick   3. make sense
4. luck   5. during   6. goods
7. boost   8. early on

[Unit 6]

Getting Ready

Page 54

C

2, 1, 5, 4, 3

D

Topic:	Geology
Introduction:	<u>S</u>tudies <u>physical aspects</u> of the Earth.
	Looks at <u>materials</u> and what happens to them.
Composition:	Earth made of <u>rocks</u>.
	Rocks made of <u>minerals</u>.
	Minerals have <u>consistent composition</u>.
Types of rocks:	<u>Three</u> types of rock.
	Different <u>textures</u> and <u>minerals</u>.
	Change via the rock <u>cycle</u>.
Study rocks to:	Geologists <u>identify</u> rocks to learn history.
	Look at changes in <u>landforms</u>.
Learn:	Learn about living things by looking at <u>fossils</u>.

Page 55

E

1. A, B, D

F

1. aspect   2. identify   3. physical
4. geology   5. consistent

Practice

Page 57

C

1. B, D, E   2. C

D

1. considerable 2. continent   3. range
4. apart   5. consequence

Answer Key

Test

Pages 58–59

1. C   2. A   3. B   4. D
5. C   6. A, C, E

Check-up

Page 60

A

1. B

B

1. melts   2. eruption   3. minerals
4. composition   5. texture   6. upward
7. landforms   8. edge

[Review 1]

Reading 1

Pages 61–62

1. C   2. D   3. A   4. B
5. B   6. A

Reading 2

Pages 63–64

1. C   2. B   3. C   4. C
5. C   6. A

Reading 3

Pages 65–66

1. B   2. B   3. B
4. C   5. C
6.

Chemical properties of gold
- (A) Made of atoms
- (D) Kind of metal
- (E) One of 117 elements

Uses of gold
- (B) Makes jewelry
- (F) Trade and coinage

[Unit 7]

Getting Ready

Page 68

C

3, 4, 2, 1

D

Topic: William Wordsworth
Introduction: Famous English <u>poet</u>.
     Born 1770 and died <u>1850</u>.
     Grew up in beautiful <u>Lake District</u>.
Poems: Wanted to <u>celebrate</u> England's beauty.
     Wrote about flowers, <u>birds</u>, lakes,
     and old <u>buildings</u>.
Philosophy: His poems caused a <u>shift</u>.
     Reacted against idea that <u>feelings</u>
     not important.
     Believed <u>emotions</u> and feelings most
     important.
Famous work: Poem called *The Prelude*.
     <u>Published</u> after his death.
     Poem tells why Wordsworth became
     a <u>poet</u>.
     Starts—He's a <u>boy</u>.
     Finishes—He's an <u>adult</u>.

Page 69

E

1. A   2. A   3. B   4. A

F

1. shift   2. approach   3. philosophy
4. celebrated   5. stated

Practice

Page 71

C

1. B   2. B   3. B, C, E

D

1. assumed   2. realize   3. pride
4. demonstrated   5. prejudice

Test

Pages 72–73

1. B   2. B   3. A   4. C
5. C   6. B, D, E

Check-up

Page 74

A

1. D   2. C

B

1. rude   2. explain   3. poet
4. District   5. prelude   6. liar
7. poem   8. novel

[Unit 8]

Getting Ready

Page 76

C

5, 1, 4, 2, 3

D

Topic:	Deforestation
Introduction:	<u>Trees</u> keep the air clean.
	Trees <u>filter</u> pollution from the air.
	The loss of trees affects the <u>climate</u>.
Negative effects:	Deforestation damages <u>animal habitats</u>.
	Many animals may become <u>extinct</u>.
Causes:	Deforestation is caused by large <u>companies</u> and poor <u>farmers</u>.
Result:	<u>Deforestation</u> results in poor air quality and loss of <u>potential</u> knowledge.
Solutions:	Don't support companies that <u>harm</u> the rainforest.
	Programs to end <u>poverty</u>.

Page 77

E

1. B   2. B   3. A   4. A

F

1. poverty   2. extinct   3. program
4. habitat   5. species

Practice

Page 79

C

1. A   2. B   3. B   4. B

D

1. fund   2. campaign   3. rely
4. consume   5. conserve

Test

Pages 80–81

1. B   2. A   3. D   4. C
5. B   6. A, C, E

Check-up

Page 82

A

1. D   2. A

B

1. filter   2. harm   3. as such
4. limiting   5. threat   6. cut back
7. rainforests   8. endanger

[Unit 9]

Getting Ready

Page 84

C

2, 1, 3, 4

D

Topic:	The Importance of Sleep
Introduction:	One <u>third</u> of our lives spent sleeping.
	Need it to <u>work</u> properly.
	Less than <u>adequate</u> = problems when <u>awake</u>.

Answer Key

Amount needed:
> Amount of sleep needed varies.
> Average is <u>eight</u> hours.

Reasons needed:
> Sleep affects <u>health</u> and well-being.
> Tired people can't <u>concentrate</u> and may become <u>emotional</u>.
> This makes it <u>harder</u> to sleep.

Effects: Lack of sleep results in <u>headaches</u> and <u>coordination</u> problems.
> Sleep makes us <u>faster and stronger</u>.
> Helps our <u>immune system</u> keep us from getting sick.

Page 85

E

1. B   2. A

F

1. concentrate   2. coordination   3. vary
4. constitutes   5. adequate

Practice

Page 87

C

1. B   2. A   3. B

D

1. involve   2. attitudes   3. negative
4. feature   5. insisting

Test

Pages 88–89

1. A   2. D   3. A   4. B
5. A   6. B, D, E

Check-up

Page 90

A

1. B   2. D

B

1. immune system   2. calories   3. well-being
4. fast food   5. disturbed   6. overweight
7. popularity   8. awake

[Unit 10]

Getting Ready

Page 92

C

2, 1, 3, 4, 5

D

Topic:	Digital Cameras
In the past:	Before <u>digital</u> cameras—purchase film, <u>load</u> it, take pictures.
	Couldn't <u>see</u> them.
Film cameras:	After taking pictures—wind up film, <u>take it out</u>, and have <u>it developed</u>.
Digital cameras:	Digital cameras <u>breakthrough</u> in <u>technology</u>.
	No film.
	Store photos like a <u>computer</u>.
Today:	Today—<u>cheap</u> and easy.
	<u>See</u> photos immediately.
	Put them on <u>computers</u>.
	Share via <u>email</u> and <u>websites</u>.
Conclusion:	<u>Consumers</u> prefer digital to film.

Page 93

E

1. B   2. A   3. B   4. B

F

1. Prior   2. consumers   3. digital
4. purchase   5. breakthrough

Practice

Page 95

C

1. B   2. B   3. A

D

1. acquire   2. primary   3. bulky
4. multimedia   5. collections

Test

Pages 96–97

1. D   2. C   3. D   4. C
5. A   6. A, C, D

Check-up

Page 98

A

1. B   2. D

B

1. memory   2. developed   3. load
4. hard drive   5. film   6. portable
7. wind   8. album

[Unit 11]

Getting Ready

Page 100

C

3, 1, 4, 2

D

Topic:	Democracy
Introduction:	<u>Originated</u> in ancient Greece. Rule by the <u>people</u>.
Details:	No <u>dictator</u>—no one with <u>authority</u> to rule over everyone.
Ancient Greece:	Ancient Greeks—practiced <u>direct</u> democracy. All <u>citizens</u> could take part. <u>Slaves</u> and <u>women</u> not citizens.
Today:	Today—<u>elect</u> representatives. They <u>represent</u> voters.

Page 101

E

1. B   2. D

F

1. governed   2. authority   3. originated
4. assembly   5. democracy

Practice

Page 103

C

1. D   2. B   3. B

D

1. branches   2. function   3. legislation
4. individual   5. Congress

Test

Pages 104–105

1. D   2. A   3. C   4. C
5. B   6. A, C, E

Check-up

Page 106

A

1. B

B

1. citizen   2. dictator   3. cabinet
4. practice   5. executive   6. Supreme Court
7. ruled   8. judicial

[Unit 12]

Getting Ready

Page 108

C

3, 2, 1, 4

D

Topic:	Body Language
Communication:	<u>Two</u> kinds—verbal and <u>non-verbal</u>.
Verbal:	Uses <u>words</u>.
Non-verbal:	Uses <u>gestures</u> and facial <u>expressions</u>. Also called body <u>language</u>. Makes up <u>fifty-five</u> percent of communication.
Positive body language:	Sends <u>happy</u> messages.

Answer Key

Examples: Smiles look <u>friendly</u>.
             Standing straight looks <u>confident</u>.
             Making eye contact gets <u>attention</u>.

Negative body language: Sends <u>bad</u> messages.

Examples: Crossing arms looks <u>angry</u>.
             <u>Frowning</u> looks worried.
             Looking down looks <u>shy</u>.
             Looking away looks <u>bored</u>.

Page 109

E

1.

Verbal communication
- (C) Communication by talking
- (D) Uses words

Nonverbal communication
- (A) Uses gestures and facial expressions
- (F) Makes up fifty-five percent of communication
- (G) Shown with the body

2.

Positive body language
- (B) Smiling
- (E) Making eye contact
- (H) Standing straight

Negative body language
- (A) Crossing arms
- (C) Looking away
- (F) Frowning
- (G) Looking down

F

1. gestures   2. nonverbal   3. confident
4. contact   5. verbal

Practice

Page 111

C

1.

They avoid
- (B) Saying words that make them stutter
- (E) Public speaking

They feel
- (A) Nervous
- (C) Stupid
- (F) Shy

2. D

D

1. awkward   2. concentrate   3. speech
4. perceived   5. public speaking

Test

Pages 112–113

1. B   2. C   3. B
4. A   5. B
6.

Should do in public speaking
- (B) Practice your speech
- (F) Study your subject
- (G) Make cards with key words
- (H) Stand straight

Shouldn't do in public speaking
- (A) Use big words
- (D) Speak softly
- (I) Speak quickly

Check-up

Page 114

A

1. A

B

1. stutter   2. impediment
3. expression   4. hard time
5. avoid   6. body language
7. communication   8. frown

[Review 2]

Reading 1

Pages 115–116

1. B   2. C   3. C   4. C
5. A   6. D

Reading 2

Pages 117–118

1. A   2. D   3. D   4. C
5. D   6. B

Reading 3

Pages 119–120

1. D   2. D   3. A
4. C   5. A
6.

Primary use of phone
- (C) Make calls
- (D) Receive calls

Optional use of phone
- (B) Listen to music
- (E) Take pictures
- (G) Personal planner